This book might change your life.

"Clear, lucid, and unbiased… a breath of fresh air on a difficult topic" – Steve Keller, Tallahassee Literary Review

"Anyone with spiritual questions should read this book" – Richard Poncy, novelist

"A brilliant interpretation of Plato's allegory"- Ron Wiggins, Palm Beach Post columnist

George Williams

Books by George Williams

How to Create a Black Hole
In Your Washing Machine
Snow on the Palms
Blackjack to Win: A Layman's Guide to
Beating the Game
This Eternal Darkness
All-American Boy
The Man on the Grassy Knoll
Strait of Hormuz
The Quest for God:
Shadows at the Back of the Cave

The Quest for God
Shadows at the Back of the Cave

George Williams

About the Author

George Williams is a motion picture producer, novelist and screenwriter living in the Palm Beaches. He has been barred from playing blackjack in Las Vegas for over twenty years and has made numerous TV and radio appearances on the subject. An active pilot, he has owned various aircraft. Since a teenager, he has played lead guitar onstage and on film and has recorded with various bands.

In between these stints, he was founder and CEO of several companies as well as a consultant to the U.S. Senate and an NASD Registered Principal. His proudest achievement, he says, was playing goal for the U.S. soccer team and shutting out the England World Cup championship team in a friendly. He is married with four children and seven grandchildren, all of whom he says are smarter than he is.

The Quest for God

Shadows at the Back of the Cave

by George Williams

Grey Knight Press

George Williams

ISBN-13# 978-0692480427   ISBN-10# 0692480420
Library of Congress Catalog # applied for

Grey Knight Press
mail@greyknightpress.com

Printed in the United States of America

Table of Contents

Introduction

In the summer of 2014, the Pew Research Center surveyed the religious beliefs of over 35,000 U.S. adults.[1] The extrapolated results indicate that of the 243 million American citizens age 18 or over, 71%, or 173 million, classify themselves as practicing Christians. Of these, 47% are Protestant or unaffiliated, while 25% identify as Roman Catholic. Protestants, for the first time, comprise less than half those claiming religious affiliation. Mainline denominations, such as Methodists and Presbyterians, are shrinking faster than evangelical churches.

Of the non-Christian 29%, 2% practice Judaism, while Buddhism, Islam and Hinduism together comprise about 4%.

The remaining 24%, or about 58 million adult Americans, classify themselves as either nothing in particular, agnostic, or atheist.

All the pro-religious numbers are down.   As recently as 2007, about 16% of Americans classified

---

[1]America's Changing Religious Landscape, Pew Research Center, May 22, 2015

themselves as non-religious. This group increased by half in seven years.

The survey also showed that of Americans raised in a traditional religion, 20% are now unaffiliated, outpacing the 4% of respondents not reared in a religious home who have joined churches.[2]

A separate Gallup Poll[3] quantifies atheists in the United States at 5%, a much lower figure than most of the world except South America and Africa. Subtracting these 12 million souls – or perhaps we should just say people - we come up with about 46 million American adults who, for one reason or another, are not committed either way.

Other surveys peg the churchless American adult population at nearly half, and growing. Another Pew study released in September 2015 reported that 77% of Catholics who have left the fold state they will not return.

Regardless of the exact numbers, the trend is clear. The pews are thinning.

This book attempts to provide guideposts for intelligent thought about God, in the hopes of assisting those undecided people who seek answers to difficult questions.

---

[2] Tribune News Service, May 13, 2015
[3] Win-Gallup Index of Religiosity and Atheism - 2012

Chapter 1 The Basic Questions

The literature is filled with books about God. Many are little more than sales pieces; they begin with a point of view and attempt to justify a particular belief or non-belief. Others are personal testimonials, heartfelt stories of lives changed by apparent instances of divine intervention, unexplained events, supernatural occurrences, small miracles. Many appeal to our emotions; some claim a moral high ground.

There are few legitimate works written in clear, relatable language as non-biased examinations of the most basic of questions:

If God exists, who is He? What's He like? What does He do all day?

What does He have to do with us, if anything?

Does He have a family?

What does religion have to do with God?

If He doesn't exist, how did we get here?

And so on.

It is in our nature as human beings to search for God. It is also in our nature to find Him. When we do, we are likely to give Him human characteristics, human motives, because that's all we know. We also are prone to believe He cares about us, and on occasion helps us through this life, and maybe keep us going somehow after death.

Life can be tough enough, and we all could use a little help from time to time.

Heal a loved one.

Let it be a nice day.

Let me win the lottery.

Help me get that promotion.

And so it goes... is anyone listening?

Many people question their faith at certain periods in their lives, usually difficult times. The more solid footing we are on – the more we know about ourselves and the world we live in – the better position we are in to arrive at reasonable answers.

It isn't always easy, though. God is not a dispassionate subject. Emotion often bests logic. Reverence can override analysis, guilt and doubt fog our thinking. Anger fuels rejection. Many of us are prisoners of our past: the twig is bent. It's easy to go with what is comfortable, what feels right, what our parents taught us. Others throw off the yoke and rebel, go the other way.

Faith of our fathers.

Faith is the belief in that which we cannot prove or know to be true. Faith, for most of us, is viewed as a positive trait to have. It requires trust, allegiance, loyalty. These are good things. Faith allures, yields much bounty: comfort, confidence, peace, and most of all, hope. The seas of life are rough to navigate alone, passage daunting. To struggle against the balmy trade winds of faith is often a stormy journey, tinged with guilt, fear and thoughts of betrayal.

It is not easy to know the demarcation between faith and blind faith, confidence and foolishness.

We're human, after all.

But it is worthwhile to try, to make an effort to sort things out. Thoughtfully, calmly, without social pressure if we can. It's certainly important enough.

How, then, to go about the quest for God?

The studies of Religion, Philosophy, Psychology and Cosmology explore these issues. Cosmogony, a word most of us are unfamiliar with, concerns itself with how the universe – or anything, for that matter, including sentient beings – initially came into existence.

We must of necessity begin with Cosmology, since these other studies are not very quantifiable. The observable universe is the only thing we can see, touch, and measure, if in a limited way, so it makes sense to acquire as much knowledge as we can in order to contemplate the existence of God. After all, if He exists, the cosmos is a grand product of His creation.

If science is not your forte, bear with the next two chapters please. You don't need to be a rocket scientist, but there are important points to be made which may change your perspective as you read further.

Chapter 2 The Nature of the Universe

An examination into the likelihood and character of God necessitates an examination of the universe, conventionally accepted as His creation. Aside from the voluminous number of particles, systems, things and oddments that populate the cosmos, its age and size yields a perspective we should have in order to consider the question of a Supreme Being. If we accept the premise that He exists and created the universe, then it behooves us to examine His masterpiece for clues as to methodology and handiwork. Another key reason is to examine the likelihood that the creation of humankind represents His highest and best life-form, and that also entails weighing the composition, size and age of the universe.

We must also consider the likelihood that the universe will one day die. If that happens, then what? Does God cease to exist? This would not fit our conventional description of the Lord, for then He is not eternal. Does He simply move on, or what? These are questions most of us haven't thought about very much. Before the acceptance of the Big Bang and the realization that the universe indeed had a beginning, the idea that the universe may have always been there (Steady State Theory) obviated these questions. Always being there was a comforting concept. A beginning, though, implies an end, now recognized as a near-certainty.[4] We will explore this further on.

And a beginning implies a creator.

The current estimate as to the age of the cosmos is 13.78 billion years, give or take[5,6]. If God exists, then, we may infer a degree of patience if indeed we are His only children. It is generally accepted that mankind, in its developed form, first appeared less than 200,000 years ago, although hominids began perhaps six million years earlier and the first human species around 1.8 million years ago.[7] Putting it another way, if mankind has been onstage for one second, the universe had existed for over nineteen hours before our curtain call.

These estimates are subject to change as science progresses, but we can reasonably say that by our measure of time He waited quite a while before birthing us into His cosmos. This could imply He had other things on His mind before us, but it is also probable His concept of time is completely different from ours. Since time can be manipulated, as is the case with black holes

---

[4] Scientists Measure Slow Death of the Universe, International Centre for Radio Astronomy Research, August 11, 2015
[5] Hubblesite reference desk
[6] Universe 101, NASA, WMAP's Universe
[7] Early Beginnings of Modern Humans, Natural History Museum, UK

and bodies of extreme density, or objects approaching the speed of light, that may well be the case.

From another point of view, that has to be the case. God, by definition, is not subservient to anything, and that includes time.

When we consider the size question, we must take into account we are dealing with the observable universe. We use the term observable universe because we cannot see, and will likely never see, distant portions of the cosmos because those far objects are expanding at an increasing rate, and that rate is greater than the speed of light. As a consequence, that light will never reach us as the net effect is one of recession; even the light is moving away from us.

You have probably been taught that objects cannot move faster than the speed of light, but suffice to say Hubble's Law allows this to occur in distant regions through expansion of the universe itself.   Objects – stars, galaxies, everything emitting light – are not moving faster than the speed of light through space, but space itself is expanding. To us, their light will simply fade away after that, as the speed of light is exceeded. This is indeed happening. We are becoming capable of observing much of everything that was soon after creation, thanks to the Hubble and other satellites, but before expansion rendered the very early cosmos invisible. As a result, we are slowly able to see less and less as our technology allows us more and more. It has been estimated that in about three trillion years, most of what we see will have faded away, provided the cosmos is still around, and recent discoveries suggest it won't be.

Best mark it all on your calendar.

At its far reaches, then, the universe is disappearing from view, at least from us and everything else in it. Given that parts of the universe appear increasingly shut off from human observation forever, it may be inferred that the cosmos was not created specifically as stage dressing for mankind. Along with the time question described above, this leads us to postulate that God had more in mind than just earth and its inhabitants if/when He created the universe.

This is a really big deal. The question becomes one of purpose: what, if anything, is the reason for the universe?

But maybe it only seems like the universe is vanishing from our gaze. Imagine, if you will, an ant on one end of a paper roll several feet long. The ant can sense a bit of food on the far end. The little creature sets out on a trek across the paper, the only way he knows to navigate in his world. Observing this, and inclined to help the small fellow, we lift the roll in the middle and fold it so that the ant is suddenly adjacent his meal. He got from here to there by taking a three dimensional short-cut, without the slightest understanding of what occurred. We manipulated his world by adding another dimension. Now compound this example by using a sheet of elastic material instead of paper, constantly being stretched faster than the ant can navigate. He'll never find his meal without help.

Space may be like that. There is not common agreement on its overall shape; it may be flat or curved or have other basic forms. Some of this has an impact on how the universe may eventually die, scientists feel, but this is beyond our level of understanding here. If, like our ant, we could get from here to there without having to traverse light years of conventional distance – i.e., the "space warp" of science fiction – or by manipulating time, or journeying through a wormhole[8], we would draw another step closer to the answers we seek.

But we're getting ahead. We cannot intelligently postulate a reason for the universe without getting a handle on its size and composition.

The size and age of the universe can be inferred from the length of time it has taken the oldest observed objects to reach us. That figure is 13.7 billion years. The light reaching us today from 13.7 billion light years away has little relation to the current location of the objects which generated that light, since they have had 13.7 billion years to move elsewhere. We can, though, through spectroscopic analysis of their red shift, determine how fast they have been moving away, and thus calculate where they are now. There is also a

---

[8] Less colloquially known as Einstein-Rosen bridges, these hypothetical shortcuts through space and time may actually exist. The theory is analogous to our ant-paper illustration, one dimensional level up.

proportional relationship between the amount of red shift and the distance from us. In this manner, we know that the objects generating the oldest observed light are now 45.7 billion light years away from here. This is the case in virtually every direction, and so the minimum diameter of the observable universe is placed at 93 billion light years – and expanding at an increasing rate.[9] This does not mean we are near the center of the universe, if there is one, because we are almost assuredly not. In fact, we are on the fringes of our own galaxy, the Milky Way, a veritable cosmic backwater. What it does imply is that all things in the universe are expanding from each other, so the point of observation is not immediately relevant. This in turn implies all things were once closer to each other and have their origins in a single point: the Big Bang. More on this a bit later.

We will need to construct some analogies to begin to fathom the immensity of the cosmos, because 93 billion light years is pretty much a meaningless concept. It is so vast that we will struggle to find anything impactful.

Let's start with this: If the observable universe was the size of the earth, our particular solar system would be the size of a large grain of sand. The sun would be perhaps $1/15^{th}$ the size of a hydrogen atom, and the earth about $1/180^{th}$ of that atom.

---

[9] Itzhak Bars, John Terning (November 2009) Extra Dimensions in Space and Time, pp 27

This still does not paint a very satisfactory picture, since we cannot really grasp the size of a hydrogen atom, much less a fraction of it. This next analogy is more visceral: if the Earth itself were as large as a grain of sand $1/100^{th}$ cm in size, the Milky Way – our cozy home galaxy - would be five million miles across. (It is estimated that the smallest speck visible to the naked eye is .1 millimeter in diameter, if it is not light-emitting.)

If instead the Sun was as large as that grain of sand, the nearby Andromeda galaxy would be 1.5 million miles away.

That is mind-boggling, and Andromeda is a close neighbor.

Our Milky Way galaxy is a big outfit in its own right, containing an estimated 300-400 *billion* stars[10]. The observable universe, the part we can see, contains an estimated 170 *billion* galaxies each containing, on average, somewhere between 100 billion and 300 billion stars each. There are some gigantic elliptical galaxies believed to contain a *hundred trillion* stars. Recent estimates put the total number of stars in the observable universe at about 70 *billion trillion*. There are easily more stars than grains of sand on all the beaches and deserts in the world.

Of course, mathematicians worked the problem, and came up with a rough estimate of 5 sextillion grains of sand on our planet, less than one tenth the number of

[10] Maria Temming, Sky and Telescope, July 15, 2014

stars in the observable universe. A sextillion the same as a billion trillion: 10^{21}, or one followed by 21 zeroes.[11]

While we still cannot get a handle on these kinds of numbers in our minds, we can begin to realize that when we get to virtually limitless quantities of anything, pretty much any anomaly becomes mathematically possible, no matter how likely or unlikely. In fact, the concept of likeliness becomes less and less relevant as our universe of numbers – in this case stars and planets – becomes larger. That is because we are not primarily concerned with percentages, but rather possibilities. If one exists, by definition many exist. If, say, one thousandth of one percent of the seventy billion trillion stars have planets, and one thousandth of one percent have life, that is 70^{11} inhabited planets in the universe. If one thousandth of one percent of planets with life have intelligent life, that is 70^6, or seven hundred thousand planets with intelligent life.

If we're off by just one power of ten, that would mean seven million planets with intelligent life. We need to keep this in the back of our minds as we explore the basic questions.

A converse is also a fascinating concept, i.e., how many grains of sand would hold all the stars, if each star were the size of a single hydrogen atom? How big a ball of sand would that make?

---

[11] Are There More Grains of Sand Than Stars? Fraser Cain, Universe Today, November 25, 2013

The answer is – way less than a single grain. In fact, the sand particle would be less than 25% of the size of a dust mote.[12] If each star were the size of a water molecule, we'd have a grand total of ten drops.

Even with these analogies, it is pretty much impossible to grasp the almost limitless difference between the very large and the very small, the few and the many.

Much of the pioneer work in determining the characteristics of the universe was done by Edwin Hubble, namesake of the orbiting telescope, at the Mount Wilson Observatory in Pasadena. In between competing in track and field and water polo as a Rhodes Scholar at Oxford, serving his country in World War I and rising to the rank of major, teaching high school, coaching basketball, passing the Kentucky bar, boxing the French national champion to a draw and dueling with a German naval officer who took exception to Hubble flirting with his wife, Hubble figured out the size and age of the universe in his spare time.

The guy was a real rock star, wasn't he?

Hubble knew that certain stars called Cepheid variables have a valuable property: their intrinsic brightness can be measured as a function of their period of pulsation. He scoured thousands of pictures taken by the observatory's Hooker telescope and finally found what he was looking for: distant Cepheid variables. By

---

[12] Fraser Cain, Are There More Grains of Sand Than Stars? Universe Today, Nov 25, 2013

measuring their apparent light against their actual brightness, Hubble could tell how far away each star was. They were as flashing highway mile markers.

This would be much like determining how far away an automobile is by measuring the apparent brightness of its headlights, when the true candlepower of the light is known. In this manner, he determined that the universe extended far beyond the Milky Way, which until that time had been thought the limit of the cosmos. Hubble calculated correctly that the farthest objects were 13.798 light years away when their light began the journey to Mt. Wilson. No older objects have been found since, except for one odd star named Methuselah, which appears maybe another half billion years older or so. Scientists are still trying to work that one out.

Many of the most distant objects are nebulae – interstellar clouds of dust, hydrogen, helium, traces of lithium and other ionized gases. This is the stuff of stars. As we would expect, we are seeing back into the universe's early days before stars coalesced from these early materials.

A second method of calculating the age of the universe is in approximate agreement with the above number. This involves analysis of ancient globular star clusters orbiting our Milky Way; detailed study measuring rate of fuel burn, brightness and other factors indicate these ancient stars formed about 13 billion years ago.

The age of the universe was not Edwin Hubble's only great discovery besides the German naval officer's wife. Using spectroscopic analysis, he measured the speed of distant galaxies by analyzing their red shift. Red shift as it pertains to light is analogous to a train horn moving toward and then away from us: then tone rises and then falls as the sound waves are at first compressed and then lengthened by the movement of the locomotive. Hubble would eventually prove that the entire universe is expanding, and that the velocities of nebulae (and every other celestial thing that can be observed) increase in proportion to the distance from us. This is Hubble's Law. It's not the galaxies rushing away from each other in static space, but rather the entire universe expanding, nebulae and clouds and dust and us and everything else as well as the space between. In this manner they are receding from us (and we from them) at a combined rate greater than the speed of light. Galaxies are not moving through space faster than the speed of light, because they can't, but at its outer limits space itself is expanding faster than light speed. This is an oversimplification of a very complex phenomenon involving general relativity, comoving distances, and a lot of other stuff we don't (and probably can't) understand. Take comfort in the fact that just by reading this paragraph you now know more than 99.9% of the world's population about the subject.

A useful way to imagine this might be to think of the universe as a balloon being inflated. Dots painted on the rubber surface would move farther away from each other, continually faster as the balloon expanded.

The discovery that galaxies farther away are moving faster than nearby "island universes" has had great implications on cosmological thinking. It had been largely thought that distant nebulae and other objects would be slowing down, primarily as a function of gravity, perhaps signaling the period of expansion was slowing or ending. This was possibly to be followed by a contraction period and perhaps another Big Bang. It became evident, though, that another force or forces are acting counter to gravity in order for expansion to speed up. The finding that gravity is not necessarily the dominant force led to the discovery of dark energy and dark matter. It might be more correct to say an awareness of what has been called dark energy and dark matter, since no one knows what these things really are.

There are other indications that what we see is not all there is. Cluster galaxy rotation curves possess anomalies. Uneven temperature distribution in hot gasses is unexplained. Visually, gravitational lensing of background objects by cluster galaxies indicates something unseen distorts gravity. This would be analogous to looking at a dime at the bottom of a shallow pool where the water is transparent, but the coin is distorted by ripples and eddies. The unseen here believed to be dark matter.

Dark matter has been postulated as a particular type of sub-atomic particle, but it's just a theory. Dark matter is mostly aloof to atomic particles in our visible universe, and does not really interact with ordinary matter. Its characteristics are inferred by observation, particularly its effects on gravitation, radiation, and the large-scale structure of the universe. Dark matter neither absorbs nor emits light. Originally postulated to explain irregular motions and occurrences in space, these forces are measured accurately enough to conclude our universe is 68.3% dark energy, 26.8 dark matter, and 4.9% atoms.[13] In other words, everything we see and know and touch – the observable universe – is less than 5% of what is really there; over 95% of the total mass-energy content of the universe is invisible.

Probably. Pretty weird, right?

So something is blowing up the balloon, and we don't know exactly what. We've called these phenomena dark matter and dark energy.

Will we ever unlock the mysteries remaining? The more we know, the more exotic it all turns out to be, and we realize we don't know very much at all. It's like those Russian nesting dolls. We struggle to open the outer shells, but many more remain inside, and the dolls are everywhere.

Will the universe continue to expand forever, unlikely as that now seems? If so, does this say anything about its Creator? Is He thus eternal as well?

Or if the universe will die, and God is real, will He die also? When?

---

[13] NASA Science/Astrophysics, NASA.gov, March 27, 2015

Or maybe He'll just create a new one. There had been some support for the Big Crunch, wherein gravity slows expansion, stops and eventually contracts back to another singularity, but science now believes another Big Bang would be impossible. The universe is too inefficient and entropic to "bounce"; indeed, the weak force would likely result in an immediate re-collapse into a giant black hole forever.[14] There would be no escape.

Many have believed the universe will indeed continue to expand forever at a continually accelerating rate, due to the actions of dark matter and dark forces. This likelihood has diminished considerably by discoveries announced in August, 2015 by GAMA, the Galaxy and Mass Assembly Project, as explained a bit further on.

The universe can go the way of Heat Death. This is the thermodynamic condition where entropy has been achieved – no more work is possible. The universe has settled into a bland soup. Stars don't form, shine or die. This can happen at an unknown temperature, and it might not be that high.

Another possibility is The Big Freeze. Stars run out of fuel, interstellar space has been swept clean of dust and other cosmic material, and all gradually grows dark.

No need to fret, at least yet: it probably won't make much difference to us.

---

[14] Guth, A.H. and M. Sher 1983. The Impossibility of a Bouncing Universe, Nature 302:505-506

These things have to do with the average density, rate of expansion, dark energy, and the shape of the universe. This is pretty heady stuff and we don't really need to grasp all of it, which hardly anyone does anyway, especially without a doctorate in astrophysics, cosmology and thermodynamics. Suffice for our purposes it is credible to assume infinite expansion for infinite time, or destruction of the universe by any of the methods noted above, or perhaps one that hasn't been postulated yet.

In other words, we haven't known a hell of a lot about what's going to happen – or at least not until the summer of 2015.

We also need to realize that the actual universe may indeed be infinite. We have no way of knowing, nor do we have a real reason to believe, that the observable universe is all there is. There may be parallel universes, multiverses, wormholes to other levels we know nothing about. All we know for now is that this place has been around for almost 14 billion years, is at least 93 billion light years in size and is growing exponentially.

Noted scientists including Albert Einstein and Steven Hawking went to extreme and awkward lengths to avoid admitting the universe had a beginning. The implication of a creator was an uncomfortable circumstance, as if a cop-out from scientific method and reasoning. To quote Christopher Isham:

"Perhaps the best argument in favor of the thesis that the Big Bang supports theism is the obvious unease with which it is greeted by some atheist physicists. At times this has led to scientific ideas, such as continuous creation (steady state) or an oscillating universe, being advanced with a tenacity which so exceeds their intrinsic worth that one can only suspect the operation of psychological forces lying very much deeper than the usual academic desire of a theorist to support his/her theory."[15]

Isham seems to have been quite correct; Einstein for one regretted wasting inordinate time trying to accommodate what appeared uncomfortable truths.[16]

*   *   *   *   *

So, again – we know quite a lot, and it all adds up to mean we don't know a damn thing.

The fact that the cosmos did have a beginning, though, is really tangential to the possibility of a creator, and only provides circumstantial evidence that God was that force. We just as well might say, well, *this* cosmos did have a beginning, and we're pretty much back to square one.

It's all pretty sophisticated stuff, and we need to keep these concepts in mind when contemplating God, including his alleged interactions with man, and the recorded history of these possible events.

---

[15] Isham, C, 1988. "Creation of the Universe as a Quantum Process", in Physics, Philosophy and Theology, A Common Quest for Understanding", Vatican City State: Vatican Observatory, p 378
[16] New Discovery Reveals Einstein Tried to Devise a Steady State Model of the Universe, John Farrell, Forbes, Feb 25, 2014

Chapter 3 The Big Bang

Cosmogony is the study of the origin of the universe: how it came into existence. It is as much a philosophical adventure as science, since we really don't know and there's not that much to study. Basic questions, such as did time exist? or did anything exist? prior to the creation are only addressed by conjecture. Interesting, but not much help.

Cosmology is the study of the universe from the instant of its creation forward. There is an incredible amount to study in the first 10^{-6} seconds alone, and it is almost miraculous that we have decoded and understood much of what happened since.

Sixty years ago, there were two primary competing theories about the origin of the universe: The Big Bang and the Steady State.[17] Steady State held that matter is continually created as the universe expands, and will continue to do so. Problems first arose with this concept when it was determined that certain objects – radio galaxies and quasars – only appeared at great

---

[17] A third alternative, plasma cosmology, had a moment in the sun but has pretty much been discounted. Like the Steady State theory, it also assumes an eternal universe.

distance, indicating they only existed far back in the universe's history. Nebulae - dust clouds and light elements, the recipe for star formation - were more numerous, as expected when the cosmos was very young. This meant the concept of an unchanging universe under the Steady State theory was disproved. The concept of an unending and predictable universe had been reassuring to some, and the alternative seemed unsettling.

The debate fizzled further when, in 1965, the presence of background microwave radiation (CMB, or Cosmic Microwave Background) was found by Bell Labs scientists to permeate the entire universe, at a level consistent with the Big Bang theory. That level is 2.726 degrees Kelvin.[18] CMB is an afterglow from the Big Bang, a residual from the superhot electron/quark soup that permeated space before things cooled down enough to permit the formation of atoms and the passage of light. This is the oldest known light in the universe, and is thought to have formed somewhere between 300,000 and 380,000 years after the Big Bang itself. It is everywhere, the still-glowing embers from the fierce furnace of creation.

While mostly a uniform phenomenon, there are subtle and incredibly small anomalies within the CMB that would fit behavioral expectations of expansion from an infinitesimally small space. These slight theoretical

---

[18] A.G. Doroshkevich and Igor Novikov, Mean Density of Radiation in the Metagalaxy and Certain Problems in Relativistic Cosmology, spring 1964

temperature variations, only one part in a hundred thousand, were eventually verified in 1992 by COBE (the Cosmic Background Explorer satellite). They are much like tiny ripples in a pond when a very small pebble is dropped, and prove necessary for the formation of stars and galaxies.

This was an impressive confirmation of theory, so much so that science now fully accepts the Big Bang as fact. Steven Hawking called it "...the discovery of the century, if not all time."

The universe had a beginning.

Just to complicate things, creation is thought not to have been a bang at all, not an explosion but rather an extremely hot, rapid expansion from what is termed a singularity, something with no volume. Singularity is a euphemism for an unexplained phenomenon, really, and there are many in the observable universe. This case refers to the infinitely dense gravitational point that came into existence somehow. This infinitesimal point, no larger than a single atom, contained all the matter, anti-matter, quarks, dark matter, dark forces, you and me, your mom and everything else that exists.

Really.

How that infinitesimal point came into being is the province of cosmogony, as we've said. There is debate whether something existed prior to the Big Bang, or even if time itself existed before the event. There is speculation on a prior state which did not include space at all. While science has charted the nanoseconds following the Big Bang all the way through plasma, star formation, and everything up until today's weather, no one has any real idea what, if anything, preceded the singularity.

Since we are fairly confident the universe sprang into existence 13.7 billion years ago, another question becomes inescapable. Most all major religions believe God is eternal, and always existed. But the universe is not eternal; it had a beginning.

Where was God 14 billion years ago?

*   *   *   *

With this knowledge of the vastness and majesty of the universe, we can begin to make certain observations about the God who created it as well as our place is the scheme of things. We can start by examining the Holy Scriptures for accuracy, since they venture into the realm of cosmology and other sciences.

Faiths that rely on the Old Testament to various degrees include Christianity, Judaism, Islam, Baha'i, Mormonism and Jehovah's Witnesses. We can observe that the Bible has difficulty straightaway. Genesis states that God created the heavens and the earth in six days, and rested on the seventh. In order to explain this anomaly, most religious scholars back off from the claim of a literal day, with the caveat that a "day" may have actually been longer than 24 hours. The problem is more thorny than that, however, because the time ratio is so far off. We have already shown that mankind's existence is not 1/7 of the life of the universe, but rather, in our example, as one second out of nineteen hours.

Earth's vegetation was created on the third day, we are told, but the Sun, moon and stars were not brought into being until the fourth day. There is poetry but no logic in this passage.

We can see the Old Testament of the Holy Bible, the cornerstone of Christianity, Judaism and to varying extents many other religions on earth, is not a literal document, and cannot be taken as such. In fact, we've seen that it runs into trouble right on the first page of the first book. We don't want to throw the baby out with the bath water, but recognize that to study the Bible seriously, we are required to proceed with caution. Poetry and inspiration, yes. Science, no.

The Bible is one book in a world with a diversity of Holy Scripture, each indigenous to its particular religion, whether Quran or Talmud or Coptic scripture or even the ravings of Scientology and which by themselves do not prove or disprove the existence of God. They do illustrate that Man will invent an Almighty Being and create a bridge to Him through revered books and create a lore about Him, all independent of the question as to whether He exists or not.

One observes that science has stridden forward at a faster pace than the writings and stories of earlier generations. It is clear we need to be *noticed*, whether we are in favor or otherwise.

Chapter 4 **Not With a Bang**

In August 2015, GAMA – the Galaxy and Mass Assembly Project – made a stunning announcement. GAMA stated that after a comprehensive study involving many of the world's largest ground based observatories as well as orbiting NASA telescopes GALEX and WISE, the evidence shows the universe has lost half its energy in the last two billion years, and thus half its brightness. GAMA measured the energy output of over 200,000 galaxies covering a broad range of wavelengths to conclude the universe is growing dark.

In other words, the house lights are dimming, and the cosmic curtain is slowly coming down.

Slowly from our reckoning of time, but perhaps astonishingly fast, considering the universe has been around 13.7 billion years and has lost half its energy in the last two billion. The universe is dying.

Most of the new energy[19] generated in the universe on a daily basis comes from two sources: nuclear fusion in stars, and the conversion of gravitational energy around massive black holes into

_____

[19] Not counting the energy left over from the Big Bang

electromagnetic energy. A smaller amount of energy is emitted on longer wavelengths by gigantic dust clouds re-radiating the energy from the stars contained within.[20] In these last two billion years, this energy, as well as new star formation, has decreased markedly.

Meanwhile, teams from Italy and the UK, after studying the accelerating expansion of the universe, have postulated that dark matter is slowly being converted into dark energy. Dark matter is thought to provide the latticework assisting the formation of new stars and galaxies, and the dramatic slowing of new star creation is apparent evidence of this phenomenon. Their calculations indicate that at the current rate CDM – cold dark matter – will have disappeared in one hundred billion years.[21]

The seemingly inescapable end result of both phenomena noted above is that the universe is indeed heading into a slow death of darkness and entropy. In a few billion years, the level of energy will drop below the threshold where new stars can be formed, and all will finally become cold, dark and empty.

It is as if the life of the universe were a big municipal firework: a bright flash followed by dazzling colors streaking across the sky in all directions, and finally dimming as the stars fall earthward leaving trails

---

[20] ESO 1533 – Organisation Release "Charting the Slow Death of the Universe", August 10, 2015
[21] Physicsworld.com, Nov 18 2014 "Is dark energy eating dark matter?"

of shimmering color. Right now, the images are becoming ghostly and one has to close his eyes to see the brightness again.

Recall how we've described the reaction of leading scientists to the concept that the universe had a beginning. This was a very unsettling concept to some. The thought that the universe is showing unmistakable signs of dying will likely be far more disturbing, especially at the rate of entropy observed.

To paraphrase T.S. Eliot:

"This is the way the universe ends
This is the way the universe ends
This is the way the universe ends
Not with a bang but a whimper."

Knowing that the cosmos had a distinct beginning and is heading for an indistinct, unromantic end will of necessity influence how we think about God as we continue through the rest of this book.

Chapter 5 Time

Earlier, we commented that God had a degree of patience to wait 13.8 billion years after creating the universe to introduce mankind, a little off the scale of Genesis. In truth, though, we have no way of knowing how God reckons time. It turns out this is an important question for a reason other than considered earlier: God, by our definition, is eternal. But the universe is not.

While the first 5.39×10^{-44} second of the Big Bang is unknown to us, we've got a pretty good handle on what followed. We have mapped the first instants of creation down to 10^{-43} to 10^{-36} seconds[22], which is when the force of gravity separated from other three fundamental forces[23] and the first elementary particles were created, immediately before cosmic inflation.

Steven Hawking and others have speculated – for that's all one can do – that time (as well as all physical laws, matter and space) did not exist prior to the creation of the cosmos. Our standard concept of the Almighty involves an eternal God, one who always existed. Since

---

[22] Luke Mastin, The Physics of the Universe, Timeline of the Big Bang, 2009

[23] Electromagnetic, strong nuclear, weak nuclear

we know the universe began 13.8 billion years ago, this notion of an eternal God must assume He is outside time, or can manipulate time.

For mankind, time is a one-directional concept: we only go in one direction. But time itself can be manipulated. Time can be slowed by approaching the speed of light, or becoming subject to near-infinite gravitational forces such as found at the event horizons to black holes. If a second dimension is added – the ability to move backward in time – certainly God can command it, and the concept of an eternal Deity becomes more viable. If God existed before The Big Bang, and time did not, He is by definition eternal.

We have no way of knowing what existed before the Big Bang, though, and it is entirely possible a prior universe or universes preceded the event. Time could have been a dimension exactly as now, or taken some other form, perhaps reckoned in another way. In this manner the concept of an eternal God may be substantiated.

*   *   *   *

So what does all this mean, these first chapters? Have we proven the existence or non-existence of God?

Well, by definition, we can never prove what isn't without a manifestation of what is. We have gained a better perspective, though. Our view is less parochial.

For now, you pays your money and you takes your choice. Let's introduce man into the equation, and see where we can go from here.

Chapter 6 Are We Alone?

If God exists, He can do anything He wants. He can dazzle or amuse us, mislead us with false clues, ignore us, vanish the planet in an instant. He could have created life throughout the universe or limited sentient beings to the planet earth. The purpose of this book, however, is to analyze these questions scientifically and logically in order to judge as intelligently as possible if He exists, and, if so, what He's like, all the while realizing our logic and reasoning may be chaff before the wind.

Popular science has long propounded the concept that we are amazingly lucky – that in the whole universe there is this one pretty blue planet with just the perfect conditions for life. Our earth is really something special and the implication is that maybe we're the only life in the entire cosmos.

The only reason this blarney would even have been dreamt up – or worse yet, still propounded, in light of what we now know - is man's overinflated ego. It is a nonsensical notion.

This thinking came about before the recent realization that there are billions and billions of planets orbiting billions and billions of stars, and the likelihood that we are the only lottery winner is mathematically impossible. Additionally, the premise to the above is that conditions must be approximately equal to ours, that is, liquid water, moderate temperature, sunlight and organic compounds.

Scientists had thought all forms of life depended on the sun for energy, primarily through photosynthesis. Life was a carbon based affair. You thought so too, probably, if you thought about it at all. Conditions on earth were perfect for our homemade chemical brew to eventually form life. Scientist scanned (and continue to scan) the universe for planets with a sweet spot that could foster life as we know it, worlds in the "Goldilocks zone." Weren't we lucky? Or weren't we blessed? How unique!

How whacky. What puffery.

This all changed – or should have changed - in 1977 because, of all things, volcanic vents. In that year, research vessels found red and white tubeworms existing on the ocean floor near hydrothermal vents. These tubeworms have no mouth, no digestive system, no anus, nothing.[24] But they are life nonetheless.[25]

These vents are created along mid-ocean ridges when magma wells up through cracks in the tectonic plates as they separate. The vents have been found at

---

[24] I think I dated someone like that in college.
[25] "Alien" Life Forms Discovered, NOAA, www.noaa.gov/features/monitoring_0209.vents.html

depths from a few thousand to maybe 23,000 feet. Vent ecosystems have developed in the super hot, mineral rich outflows. The hot magma leaks through cracks and heats the surrounding water near the boiling point.

But wait a minute. There's no sun anywhere around. No solar energy, no light, no nothing. So what happens?

To everyone's astonishment, it was determined that vent ecosystems derive their energy from chemosynthesis, not photosynthesis. It seems that both methodologies use carbon dioxide and really hot water as energy to produce sugars, although chemosynthesis can use methane. Photosynthesis gives off oxygen as byproduct, while chemosynthesis produces sulfur. This was all brand new and mind-boggling in 1977.

So what does it all mean? Well, if all we have to do is look down about one mile on our own planet to find a completely different ecosystem, a system based on nothing we believed could support life, what do you think the odds are that life exists elsewhere in the observable universe based on photosynthesis or chemosynthesis or quarks or strangelets or pbj sandwiches or God knows what else, in 170 billion galaxies each containing an average of 300 billion stars and an almost infinite number of planets? All in a universe of over 93 billion light years?

Even allowing for life similar to ours, new possibilities are being discovered almost routinely. The Astrophysics Journal publishes research derived from

NASA's ongoing mission to find habitable planets with the Kepler space telescope, launched in 2009. In January 2015, for instance, the U.K. Daily Mail reported that eight new candidates were unearthed – pardon the pun – where oceans may exist and sunlight is roughly equivalent to earth's.[26] Also in January, the Kepler device discovered its 1,000[th] planet.[27] In July 2015, another similar planet made the nightly news. See where it's all going?

Probably the last nail in the coffin of this ridiculous argument was driven home on September 28, 2015 when NASA announced the discovery of liquid water on the surface of Mars.[28] It seems that even our next door neighbor shows signs of life. Can any reasoning person harbor any doubt?

We are not alone. It's a mathematical and scientific certainty, but for various reasons we don't hear that much about it. It may make us uncomfortable to think we don't occupy center stage, but there it is. Not only do we have company, it's got to be in every corner of the cosmos.

---

[26] Harvard-Smithsonian Centre for Astrophysics in Cambridge, U.S.
[27] Mike Wall, Space.com, January 6, 2015
[28] "Scientists Point to Liquid Water in New Photos of Mars", NY Times, Sept 28, 2015

Chapter 7 Evolution, Creationism or Intelligent Design?

Evolution teaches that life mutates over time; beneficial mutations survive and the less adaptive ones don't. It's all a fluid, ongoing process. And it is true – we have seen and observed this in many life-forms. Mutations occur as a natural hiccup. As you know, creatures with short life spans like fruit flies are used to study and understand generational changes. We can, and have, caused rapid genealogical evolution through environmental manipulation.

Intelligent Design teaches the natural world is so complex and sophisticated it had to have a creator, but does not speculate who or what.

Creationism teaches that God created the universe and everything in it, much of it on an as-is basis. The proponents of creationism range from those deranged believers who think the earth is flat and but a few thousand years old[29] to a less literal interpretation of the

---

[29] How these people explain away the fossil record is a matter for psychiatry.

Bible; these "Old-Earth" believers allow for some evolutionary processes.

The above is an oversimplification and the truth is all three overlap. For instance, many Christians believe evolution occurred but that the human soul was imbued by God into man somewhere along the line.

Visual evidence of Intelligent Design is compelling. So-called "walking stick" insects are incredible copies of twigs and sticks. Octopus and other animals change color, shape and texture to disappear amid their surroundings. Squid, chameleons, cuttlefish and others vanish in plain sight. How can they possibly do that? There are countless other examples of incredible adaptations. We've already noted the bizarre life forms that sprang up around undersea volcanic vents. Did all these things just evolve? Is there really a blind watchmaker?[30]

To quote Jeff Goldblum in *Jurassic Park*, "Life finds a way."

Perhaps, but when one views these amazing creatures it is very easy to believe they are products of Intelligent Design, and not just hundreds of generations that finally "got it right".

The problem, though, is that we have a mountain of evidence for unintelligent design, apparent mistakes littering the geological record. Weighing against Intelligent Design are the countless examples of dead-

---

[30] The Blind Watchmaker, Richard Dawkins, Norton & Co, 1986. A powerful argument making the case for evolution without design.

end life-forms that didn't make it, as any evolutionary biologist can attest. Exacerbating this natural process, we are currently experiencing extinction at a rate not seen since the dinosaurs were wiped off the earth 65 million years ago.   It is estimated that 200 species *per day* are becoming extinct.[31] These numbers are contested, and other estimates vary wildly, since no one really knows. The only thing they all agree on is that man's actions are responsible for the great increase in extinction of species, primarily through destruction of environment but also because of deliberate killing.[32]

We've noted that many religions have a hard time with evolution for reasons which have little logic. There is no reason to believe a creator would not have let life evolve as it will.   In fact, there have been so many bizarre life-forms[33] and dead-end species, it's hard to conceive of these being intelligently designed unless God was just doing it for unknown reasons, maybe just tinkering around. By definition, then, they wouldn't be mistakes, would they?

Since He waited 13.7 billion years to put us into the mix, He wouldn't seem to have been in a big hurry. For irrational reasons, evolution is an abhorrent concept to certain people, including, no doubt, the KKK.

---

[31] UN Environment Programme:200 Species Extinct Every Day Since Dinosaurs Disappeared 65 Million Years Ago, Manchester Guardian, August 17, 2010

[32] Yet another manifestation of man having been created "in God's image".

[33] Like my brother.

Chapter 8 How Big is God?

The short answer is a hell of a lot bigger than we ever gave Him credit for, if indeed He exists at all. Our conception of the Almighty has lagged behind our discoveries of the vastness, wonder and complexity of His dominion.

A preceding chapter postulating the certainty of life in the universe is really a prelude to this question. I'll say right off I do not know if God exists, and neither do you or anyone else, no matter what they say or wear. We can believe He's real, and most do, but we must recognize that belief is not necessarily knowledge.

Personally, I'd like to think He's really there. If so, there are things we can say about Him against the backdrop of knowing a bit about the observable universe. Some of these things are at odds with accepted beliefs as put forth by organized religion. If you're going to make up your mind about God, though, you should do it with the aid of some sort of intelligent factual basis. Again, that's the point of this book.

Faith does not preclude reason. For many of us, unfortunately, our thought processes shut off Sunday mornings. We toddle off to worship, singing the old songs that give us comfort, retelling the stories we've heard since childhood, repeating by rote the prayers of our ancestors. And, by themselves, they do us no harm. In fact, an hour or so thinking higher thoughts, or at least lolling away the time without electronic devices, doesn't hurt anybody. Maybe we give a mental shrug and go along, while in the back of our minds we push aside doubt.   But some will push aside the homilies and gospels and rituals and ask new questions.

As we learned, if the earth were the size of a grain of sand, our galaxy would be about five million miles across, a hell of a trip in the family minivan. And the Milky Way is but one of the 170 billion galaxies we know about, each containing on average 300 billion stars and a virtually infinite number of planets. We can't really begin to fathom it.

This kind of knowledge yields a new perspective, one that would have been impossible when virtually all religions were formulated. Does it make a lot of sense to believe God created the whole entire shebang, this impossibly rich, immense and diverse Grand Stage, with all its nova, dark matter, black holes, strangelets, quarks, solar systems, companion stars, comets, meteors, red giants, white dwarfs, cosmic rays, nebulae, brown dwarfs, neutron stars, main composite stars, radio galaxies, pulsars, gamma ray stars, dust clouds and everything else just for our benefit, stage dressing for an infinitesimal speck off in a dusty corner of an out-of-the-way galaxy?

Maybe. As we said before, He can do anything
He wants. But is it likely?

Once we begin to realize the grandeur and
immensity of the universe in which we are not even a
speck, the amount of attention religion assumes we get
from our Creator seems an enormously egotistical
concept. We are making God awfully small, almost a
lighting technician on a very small stage. In our view of
the Almighty, it seems we haven't progressed very much
since Ptolemy postulated a geocentric universe around
110 AD, because we still believe it, at least on Sunday.
We *really* want to be the center of attention, if the center
of nothing else. It is more plausible to posit that He
oversees a near-infinite variety of life in lots and lots of
places in His universe. That makes more sense, right?
He's on a vastly more cosmic, majestic scale if He's
anything at all. Our universal crime is trivializing the
Lord of Creation, if we choose to believe in Him.

Of course, we can get around the problem by
assigning Him all-knowing and all-seeing attributes.
Given the case, He can oversee life everywhere at once,
and attention to all is paid. And maybe that's so. But
again, is it likely?

It's a lot easier to toddle off to worship, sing the
old songs, retell the stories and repeat the prayers. But
we're starting to think. For some of us, it's a new
activity, and hopefully won't generate a headache.

Chapter 9 Where is God?

The concept of an all-seeing, all-knowing God implies that He is everywhere. But is He really big and huge?   A ludicrous concept, probably, but where is everywhere?   Or perhaps more interesting, where was everywhere? If God exists outside the universe, where is that? Or *is* God the universe?

Let's go back to the beginning, at least the beginning of this universe. Immediately following the Big Bang, the cosmos was charged with positively charged nuclei and negative charged electrons. The whole place was ionized. This blocked light from traveling, and the universe was dark.[34]

This blackout lasted for about 400,000 years, after which the cosmos had cooled sufficiently for atoms to form and allow light to pass. This first light, the light of birth from the Big Bang, lit the universe. This glow gradually faded until darkness again enveloped all[35]. Cosmic night then prevailed for maybe four hundred

---

[34] How Did the First Stars and Galaxies Form?, Abraham Loeb, chairman, Princeton U Astronomy Dept, Princeton U Press, 2010

[35] As we've seen, the residual light is still with us at 2.76 degrees K

million years, after which the first stars formed and began to shine.[36] So: dark, light, dark, light.

During the long cosmic darkness, then, where was God? Was he outside the universe, perhaps? It doesn't seem likely he was *in* the universe, does it, doing God-knows-what in total darkness? Even given the premise that time to Him is meaningless or manipulated?

It leads us to the idea that God is not a specific locus, doesn't it? If indeed he has a location, it well could be outside the universe. Now that makes sense, because he would have to be outside the universe to have created it, wouldn't he?

That's a really interesting thought. For God to be somewhere inside the universe now, wouldn't He have had to move inside it after creating it? When would He have done that? Why? Interesting thoughts leads to intriguing questions. If heaven exists, then, where is it? What about hell? Could they have anything to do with dark matter? Dark energy?

It tends us to postulate that perhaps God is a force, without dimension, a conceptualization, so that location has no meaning, which also makes sense from the standpoint that matter may not have existed prior to the Big Bang.

Now these may seem obvious points but really they must not be, because we continually conceive of

---

[36] The Universe's Dark Ages: How Our Cosmos Survived, Clarence Choi, Space.com, Oct 24, 2011

God as a floating man[37] in a robe, light streaming from him, glowing halo overhead. Right?

So what this means is that all those book markers and book jackets and old paintings showing a kindly haloed man with kindly eyes and a wise hand gesture in a flowing robe are undoubtedly cartoons. In fact, when we think about it, the robe and halo are ridiculous concepts, another indication as to how we humanize God to try and relate to Him.

We also speculated that God could actually *be* the universe. It's not an impossible idea, and it doesn't necessarily imply He had a beginning. We've already noted the Big Bang could be an event in a sequence, bursting forth as a force of impossible energy from whatever was before.

It would have been a hell of a grand entrance.

---

[37] Some think God is a woman. Even the Bible doesn't think that.

Chapter 10   The Discomfiture of the Near-Infinite

Given the near-certainty of life in abundance throughout the universe, new dilemmas confront us. Many religions hold that God in some form visited earth, sometimes with adverse consequences. This is particularly worrisome for Christianity, which states that The Son of Man was sent by his Father to save the human race by dying on the cross. He was God's only Son, we are advised, so things seem painted into a corner, and a very small corner at that. With the assumption of life everywhere, intelligent life throughout the cosmos, was Jesus sent anywhere else? Did he have many mothers? Was or is it his job to die a multitude of deaths on a multitude of planets that need salvation? This does not sound appealing. It doesn't sound likely, either. In fact, it sounds nuts. So what are the implications of this?

One must balance the size, age and complexity of God's grand creation against the story of the sacrifice of his only Son on this planet, an infinitesimal mote. It is a troublesome contemplation.

All the world's major religions were formulated well before the size and scope of the universe were realized. Many of the concepts promulgated by creaky theological dogma seem outdated, unrealistic, quaint. Creation of the stars in Genesis is treated as turning on house lights for God's earth show. Alleged miracles seem dated, almost sideshow-like, as for instance the wiggling of the sun at Fatima, the burning bush in the desert, the large fish catch by the apostles. There are far more spectacular sights on television and in the theater, especially with the advent of CGI. The old-time miracles would be yawners to the second graders of today.

Maybe God matched the miracle to the sophistication of the times, though.

Some devout scientists struggle to fit the observable universe and its characteristics, including its birth and likely death, into religious molds that seem anachronistic. Einstein's wasted calculations, previously cited, are an example. Again, if He exists, He can do anything He wants, no matter how it seems to us, but we must continue the struggle to weigh the evidence and hope to arrive at outcomes that don't leave us worrying at night. This may not be entirely possible for intelligent and logical people.

Chapter 11 My Fish Tank

I have a tank with a variety of salt water fish. I
suppose I am their god, in a way, although I didn't create
them. Some have beautiful and vivid color schemes, as
if painted by Picasso on living canvas. Did God do that?
I wonder.

I did create and control their environment, setting
the timer for light and dark, arranging the rocks and the
sand, populating their little watery world. I've created
their entire cosmos, haven't I? It took me about a week,
too. Do they have any concept that there's a universe
outside their 90 gallon home? Perhaps at night, when the
tank is dark and household night lights appear like
faraway stars to the little creatures.

And they are aware of me, I know, for when they
see me coming at feeding time they swim excitedly. The
food trickles down, manna from heaven.

Is there any concept of how their world came into
being? Do they gaze at the filter intake and wonder
where the water goes? What happens to it? Any
thoughts about their deity? What I think, what I do? It's
ludicrous to even pose these questions, but there is an

analogy here.   It's likely just as hopeless for us to envision our Creator - what He thinks, what He does. We have fewer frames of reference than the fish – they can see me coming.

On occasion, I have accidentally introduced a fish that is a predator for another inhabitant. Cain slays Abel. I can banish the killer – last time it was a triggerfish – for the sake of all the inhabitants of the tank. I can interfere with the natural course of events.   Most animals and some fish kill for food. Some, like the triggerfish, are naturally aggressive, territorial. It is the way of life he knows. Do I interfere? As the Fish Tank God, I make a value judgment to remove the offending fish, leave him be or perhaps banish him to a smaller, separate tank, away from the watery Garden of Eden. The remaining population may not notice he's gone. Would I punish him for acting as he was made? Would I not feed the rest of the fish, make them forage for scraps of algae among the coral?

It was my fault, certainly, for introducing an aggressive species into a serene world of butterfly and angelfish. Can I blame the trigger?

Can God blame Adam or Eve? Didn't he create the snake that tempted them? That idea doesn't seem to have worked out. Whose fault is that?

It is my natural inclination to interfere, protect my fish. And I did not even create the creatures.

If God exists, then, and watches what goes on here on earth, His thoughts are very different from mine.

It seems as though He doesn't fix much, at least anymore, as far as we know. Perhaps He lost interest. Perhaps He gave us up as too flawed, more an insult to His image than a likeness. Perhaps He was more successful with another planet(s) somewhere else in the cosmos, where the inhabitants don't kill and persecute each other endlessly in His name.

It is easy to judge, harder to try and understand and refrain from judging.

This is not really possible, though. Christianity and Judaism, though possessing a common beginning, differ markedly on many things, including the temperament of God. Christ, divine or not, held that the Almighty is a Loving God. Protestants in particular came to believe He wants a 'relationship' with each of us, although the word itself never appears in the Bible. It seems a misnomer, a grotesque assumption, another gigantic ego trip. What is it supposed to mean? Is God lonely? The nature of this relationship is only vaguely stated, involving worship and freeing ourselves from sin. Is that a relationship? Isn't a relationship characterized by give and take? How Protestants arrived at this logic seems fuzzy.

The concept of worship is not clear cut, in any event. There is occasional debate among Christians, for example, as to whether it is our purpose to worship God or if He wants to be adored at all.

I don't want the fish in my tank to worship me. Even if they could, I don't need the adulation. We can't have a meaningful relationship. They will do what they will do. One day my fish tank world will end. The tank may spring a leak, or if the whole apparatus is moved it would need to be emptied and drained. But I will go on. To the fish, then, I am eternal.

Chapter 12 String Theory and M-Theory

There has, of necessity, been a scientific bent to the first chapters in this book and the hope is that a greater understanding of the universe we live in provides a better perspective when considering the likelihood of a Supreme Being. Before moving into other areas, though, it is necessary to present a brief overview of string theory and its subsequent refinement, M-theory.

String theory has been around for a couple of decades and, if correct, would have a profound impact on much of what we have described so far and how we weigh the concept of God. It is unproven, and therefore we have not considered this possibility as we have gone along because string theory provides radically different answers to the key questions we ask concerning the nature of things. To do so would have complicated matters and caused unnecessary confusion and so it is dealt with in this chapter alone.

The universe contains four distinct forces with defined physics of behavior:

1. Gravity

2. Electromagnetic force (electricity and magnetism)
3. Strong nuclear force (binding atomic nuclei)
4. Weak nuclear force (radioactive decay)

While behavior of these forces and their interactions are generally well understood, the fact is that the physics of these break down in at least two instances: the center of black holes, and the first instant of the Big Bang. Moreover, the laws of quantum physics were created to describe particle phenomena otherwise unexplainable by conventional means. It is also safe to say no one really understands quantum mechanics, the theory of the very small.

It's all a bit messy.

String theory postulates a single unifying formula to explain all phenomena and therefore has been dubbed the "theory of everything." Basically, it says that all subatomic particles – and now there are thousands - are composed of energy strings, either closed in irregular circles or open. These strings vibrate at varying rates, producing the vast array of subatomic particles depending on the rate of vibration. This is much like guitar strings producing different notes depending on where the strings are pressed to the fretboard. The string is the same, the resultant notes are different. In string theory, the strings are the same, the vibrations differ, and thus the resultant particles are different.

So what? This entire chapter would be but an esoteric exercise if string theory didn't postulate some startling concepts. Without a treatise on the matter, suffice to say string theory propounds the existence of eleven dimensions, instead of the three we know, and allows for parallel "membranes", or universes, nicknamed branes. It is theorized that whenever these parallel universes collide, or even barely touch – BANG!

Thus, the concept goes, our universe was created from a Big Bang caused by two membranes, or parallel universes, brushing each other at a infinitesimally small point. As these membranes float about, this phenomenon will possibly repeat at intervals so that – again – another Big Bang could occur.

The stuff of science fiction? Sure. It all sounds pretty crazy, but so far the math can't be disproven. Perhaps in another decade string theory will be accepted or discarded. The only thing we should take away from all this is the concept that everything may be much larger than we have thought, and that's pretty large anyway, and indeed the universe(s) may have always existed and the Big Bang is an occasional occurrence.

If God exists, and string theory is accurate, He's *really* much bigger than we thought, and his kingdom is infinitely vaster than we imagined, and it may well have been around forever, and may last forever, and we are an impossibly small component of the whole affair.

Chapter 13 The Concept of Worship

Giving thanks to God is a common and praiseworthy practice, and takes many forms. Man has a lot to be thankful for, starting with his very existence, and he often acknowledges it through prayer, economic support of religious organizations, charity and the like.

Thanks for healing a loved one.

Thanks for a nice day.

Thanks for letting me win the lottery.

Thanks for helping me get that promotion.

And so on.

Worship, as we touched on in the previous chapter, is more encompassing. Virtually every civilization has created or discovered its God, or gods, and worship forms the central theme to the relationship. It is an unquestioned practice, but perhaps we should explore why mankind approaches his maker through worship.

In its most ethical sense, worship is an extreme form of respect. God is worshipped because He created the worshipper and everything else, and it is natural for His creations to feel He deserves respect and admiration for having done so. Whether He appreciates the gesture or not, it is a nice thing to do.

On a lesser plane, God is often worshipped to get on His good side, to curry favor or get something from Him. This often implies taking something away from someone else, such as his life.

Worship has taken strange forms. Man kills his fellow man in battle and ritual, and innumerable animals as well, in the strange belief this is somehow pleasing to God, who created not only the killer but the slain. In its most extreme and grotesque form, the Arabic phrase "Allahu Akbar" – God is great - has been shouted out while beheading hogtied victims, sometimes onscreen. It is difficult for the Western mind, or any sane mind, to reason how this could somehow be pleasing to the Almighty.

Psychotic or respectful, all concepts and forms of worship stem from the human point of view. Is there any reason at all to think God wants to be worshipped? Against the backdrop of the magnificence of the universe, his creation, it seems hard to believe God needs adulation from us. Why would he want it from anyone or anything, much less something as insignificant in the cosmos as mankind? Again, this appears another example of man's bloated ego.

The Bible attempts to explain this concept in several places. Exodus 20:3 quotes God: "Thou shalt have no other gods before me."

A bit further in Exodus 30:5 we find this strange, startling passage: "Thou shalt not bow down thyself to them, nor serve them: for I the Lord am a jealous God, visiting the iniquity of the fathers upon the children unto the third and fourth generation of them that hate me..."

Wow.   That's nuts, right? It is difficult to conceive anyone could take this passage – a *really* vengeful God admitting to a sinful trait - seriously.   To continue:

Kings 17:36: "But the Lord, who brought you up out of the land of Egypt with great power and a stretched out arm, him shall ye fear, and him shall ye worship, and to him shall ye do sacrifice."

As we know, sacrifice is a popular topic in the Old Testament.

And further:

Revelation 3:9: "Behold, I will make them of the synagogue of Satan, which say they are Jews, and are not, but do lie; behold I will make them to come and worship before thy feet, and to know that I have loved thee."

A strange passage in Revelation, a book of strange passages.

And in 13:8: "And all that dwell upon the earth shall worship him, whose names are not written in the book of life of the Lamb slain from the foundation of the world."

The best we can say is that the Bible promotes worship and attributes the practice to God's wishes, but the verses are so tainted with illogic they can only be cited for historical reasons.

The reasonable conclusion is that man created worship and justifies it on his own. Much of the time it is a sincere and uplifting practice, and much of the time it is self-serving. We can assume God, if He's there, knows the difference.

Chapter 14 **Common Sense**

Thomas Paine's treatise on the subject of religion, *The Age of Reason*, was an early investigation into the character and nature of God. Initially published in 1794, Paine begins by professing his belief in one God and no more, a belief he tests in the ensuing pages. The book was largely written in Luxembourg Prison, where he was being held in France after being convicted of betraying the state[38]. Widespread publication did not occur in England for several years thereafter, as the volatility of his musings were not in the public interest. In America, though, the cheap pamphlet became a bestseller and fueled popular debate. Paine by that time had returned to America, where he was called the anti-Christ by those who took exception to his writings. The story didn't end well, as he died broke in New York.

Paine was a believer in Deism, which holds that through logic, reason and observation man arrives at the conclusion there is a single God. Speaking for many of the intellectuals of his day whom had become disenchanted with Christianity as an organized entity,

---

[38] The Age of Treason?

Paine rejects the supernatural events of the Bible, as well as the Holy Trinity and biblical inerrancy; that is, the notion that the Bible is an infallible book that preserves without error God's teachings. Deism states that God does not interfere with the workings of the natural world. It believes in the evolutionary process rather than intelligent design.

In other words, once God created the universe, he left it alone.

Paine went further, declaring that the major organized religions – Jewish, Catholic or Turkish, as he called them – were "human inventions set up to terrify and enslave mankind, and monopolize power and profit." Paine then bitterly denounces those individuals who exhibit "professional belief" but who have "corrupted and prostituted the chastity of (his) mind." He aims his arrows at priests, many of whom, he avers, take up the trade for the sake of gain.

As we might imagine, it didn't take but a few hours before he was thrown in the clink.

Paine, whose pamphlet *Common Sense* had swayed a significant number of colonists to break from English rule, observed several commonalities among the major religions. In each case, he states, the religion was established to perform a special mission from God communicated privately to certain individuals. Paine was a trifle inflammatory on this point, and didn't mince his words.

He cites the Jews' belief that the Word of God was given to Moses face to face, the Christians' position that the Word of God was brought about by divine inspiration, and the Quran brought to Muhammad by an angel from heaven.

Here are two paragraphs worth quoting from Paine's insightful work:

"Every national church or religion has established itself by pretending some special mission from God, communicated to certain individuals.   The Jews have their Moses; the Christians their Jesus Christ, their apostles and saints; and the Turks their Mahomet; as if the way to God was not open to every man alike.'

'Each of these churches shows certain books, which they call *revelation*, or the Word of God.   The Jews say that their Word of God was given by God to Moses face to face; the Christians say their Word of God came by Divine inspiration; and the Turks say, that their word of God (the Koran) was brought by an angel from heaven.   Each of these churches accuses the other of unbelief; and, for my own part, I disbelieve them all."

Paine then goes on to say that these revelations were passed from God to man in an immediate sense, that is, one on one. All others who believe these tenets do so based on hearsay, and further, hearsay upon hearsay. He concludes by saying that as hearsay, he is not obliged to believe any of it.

Of course, neither Paine nor you and I are obliged to believe any of it, nor do we have to believe Paine. Then again, we probably don't share his vitriol.

The philosopher/theorist/revolutionary makes several interesting points, though. It is troublesome to envision God, almost as someone peeking out of a hiding place, whispering "Hey, buddy" and revealing something of cosmic import to an individual. The revelations may be true, but are conveniently not subject to verification. No grand announcement to the multitudes, no epic appearances, no stupefying supernatural stunning occurrences, no real proof. Rather, poetic encounters shrouded in mystery.

Hmm.

Chapter 15 Religions of the World

There is logic that says the last place to look if one wishes to learn about God would be organized religion.

Studying religion in an effort to contemplate God is a bit like scrutinizing the fans of FC Barcelona to understand why the club is the best soccer team on earth (although Premier League aficionados might disagree). We can learn things about the followers of the club and fans of the players, marvel at their fanatical devotion, but this has little to do how the team works and why the club consistently reigns at the top of the world soccer stage, FIFA scandals notwithstanding.

The really avid soccer fans are somewhat unbalanced, but it doesn't mean the players are. Religion tells us much about the worshipers of God, and very little about God himself, as we shall see.

Religions are indigenous to human existence. Belief in an Almighty has been a cornerstone of virtually every civilization since mankind stood erect. It cannot be eradicated by totalitarian regimes, even under the draconian rule of such countries as Cuba, Cambodia, or the old Soviet Union, all of whose prohibitions were eventually washed away by the tide of faith. You already know all this.

That said, it is interesting to note certain characteristics and trends in the world today.

Overall, religiosity in the world has dropped by 9% in the seven years between 2005 and 2012. Atheism rose by 3%.[39]   Of those who identify themselves ethnically or sociologically with religious groupings, 54% of Jews proclaim themselves non-religious by a much wider margin than any other group; Christian non-religious responders were 16%, Muslims 20% and Hindus but 12%.

A lot of Jews don't want to be Jews, it seems.

The 2012 Win-Gallup religious study revealed that religion is most practiced by the poor. The numbers by quintile are:

Bottom – 66% religious
Low - 65%
Medium – 56%
Medium-High – 51%
High Income - 49%

The same study shows religious belief declines in proportion to education:

Less than secondary education – 68% religious
Secondary education – 61%
Higher education – 52%

---

[39] Win-Gallup International Global Index of Religiosity and Atheism-2012

The poor and uneducated believe, the well off and educated, not so much. Is this surprising?

Religion is a free possession, and often about the most the poor can afford. It is also invaluable, if faith is based on truth, and perhaps even if not. Religion is thus equated with hope. The well off have stuff and can enjoy the worldly, and don't need the emotional comfort of religion so much, at least until things go wrong in life. The uneducated lack the tools of perspective and analytical thinking, the ability to evaluate and compare.

Again, all the above has virtually no bearing on our basic question: Is God real?

There are hundreds and hundreds of belief systems in the world today, ranging from small cults to the major religions. It is a sad but true fact that there are always people who will believe anything; the cult of personality has proven incredibly strong, beyond at times even the instinct to live. The most extreme examples such as Jonestown (The People's Temple), Waco (Branch Davidians) and Scientology speak for themselves. Instructing over a thousand people to commit suicide and kill their children by drinking poisoned Kool-Aid® or perishing in a fire and having them actually do it is at the limit of comprehension.

Cults can be distinguished by the following characteristics:

- Extreme child abuse (bruising, beatings, isolation)

- Beatings of disobedient members
- Severe food deprivation as punishment
- Outside family ties severed
- Sleep deprivation of members
- Use of fear and intimidation to coerce obedience
- Isolation from ex-members[40]

Certainly Waco and Jonestown exhibited all the above; an explosive 2015 HBO television documentary[41] portrays Scientology as falling into this category.

Aside from these extreme and aberrant examples, it is instructive to examine a sampling of the religions representing most of humanity. The group includes Christianity and its various offshoots (2 billion), Islam (1.3 billion), Shinto (100 million), Hinduism (950 million), Buddhism (350 million) and Judaism (14 million).

Christianity, Islam and Judaism all have experienced major fractures over their histories, some bitterly so. Catholic and Orthodox split in 1054, Catholic and Protestant in the 1500s. Islam broke into Shia and Sunni sects, with about 90% identifying themselves as Sunni. They kill each other to this day. Judaism calved into Reformed and Orthodox. None of these appear likely to reconcile.

---

[40] Christian Research Institute, 2015, Article ID:DD0025
[41] Going Clear:Scientology and the Prison of Belief, 2015

There are probably thirty or so other religions with sizeable followings. Some believe in multiple gods. Christianity, Islam and Judaism are conventionally seen as monotheistic, but Christianity really is a hybrid because of the belief in three Gods of various levels, i.e., the Holy Trinity.

Several believe in an afterlife, and about an equal number believe in reincarnation. Others such as Confucianism[42] or Deism do not address the subject at all, stressing a lifestyle.

A very few such as Epicureanism deny an afterlife. Of the more bizarre beliefs, Jehovah's Witnesses confine Heaven to a specific number.[43] Some Jews divide Hell by temperature, as we shall see.

Religion relies heavily on ritual, often elaborate. Ritual combines mysticism, the comfort of repetition, the sense of historical importance and holy origin. All these contribute to feelings of validity and purpose; they help fulfill man's need for God. In reality, ritual neither confirms nor impugns the basic question of God's existence; in fact, nothing man does confirms or repudiates His existence. It does, however, give rise to the question of Holy interference in earthly events.

Christianity, Judaism, Islam and many other religions are filled with descriptions of God's interplay

---

[42] Technically not considered a religion.
[43] The claim of 144,000 is based on Revelation 7 and 14, but ignores the fact that the saved are described as being from the 12 tribes of Israel, effectively shutting out the practicing Jehovah's Witnesses from salvation.

with life on earth, a practice largely abandoned by Him when mankind achieved a level of sophistication where communication methods were improved and verification became a factor. Christianity seems to acknowledge the waning of heavenly activity on earth by claiming the birth and sacrifice of Jesus obviated the need for much more celestial interference.

There are, of course, sporadic claims of miracles in the world today. One of the most well-known occurred on October 13, 1917, outside Fatima, Portugal. Unlike past supernatural interactions, which had been largely limited to one-on-one events, somewhere between 30,000 and 100,000 persons had gathered to see if a solar prediction given to three young shepherd children would come to pass. Indeed, many people affirmed seeing the sun perform strangely, ranging from rapid circular movements to color changes to an appearance of rushing toward the earth. These claims were investigated in some detail by reporters who interviewed many of the attendees, and in due time the sun's gyrations were deemed a miracle by the Roman Catholic Church. As might be expected, there are many detractors who explain what seemed to have occurred as mass hysteria, a sun dog, effects on the retina of staring at the sun, too much grappa, and pretty much anything else that could possibly be involved.

Unless a miracle of stupendous proportions occurs in the future, it is likely that any other happenings will be discounted by virtue of the fact that computer generated imagery (CGI) can make anything seem possible, as any moviegoer over the age of three can attest.

Delving into the details of various faiths is not our purpose here.   There are many publications and websites with charts and statistics that describe and compare most of the religions practiced around the world. We don't need to duplicate them in this book. The few examples we have examined so far lead to the conclusion that religion is not going to give us much of a handle on God, but rather insights into the psyche of mankind.   Religion represents the best of us and it represents the worst of us.   It has been said that more people have been killed in the name of God than for any other reason, and certainly this is a way of life in areas such as the Middle East and parts of Africa. Losing ourselves in the details of religion is counterproductive to our goal; we will not learn much about God or gain insight into whether He exists.   It is unfortunate that the basis of much religion in the world today is typified by the expression "We're in, you're out."

It is easy to take potshots at almost any religion; all have rituals and beliefs that seem ludicrous to those outside the particular faith.   Unless the purpose is to wean an individual away from a specific religion – not the intent here – there isn't much purpose in listing some of the more bizarre articles and practices of the world's religions.   Most have inherent problems, though, beyond the superficial and require a dogged faith to sustain their adherents.

In the next chapters, we'll take a brief overview of Christianity and Judaism, if for no other reason that we live in what has been labeled a "Judeo-Christian society" and we are all somewhat familiar with the tenets and practices of these faiths.

Chapter 16 Problems with Christianity

Christianity and its many branches, sects and divisions together form the largest religious grouping in the United States, although Protestantism is gradually declining.   The Pew study described in Chapter One indicates that for the first time Protestant membership has dipped below 50% of religions in the United States. It may be misleading to aggregate all who believe in Jesus as mankind's savior under one banner, because they differ in considerable measure, sometimes wildly so, and often are at verbal or civil war with each other. Upheavals and disputes are common even within certain branches; for instance, the recent schism between Presbyterians has resulted in property disputes as well as spiritual differences. The role of women in the various denominations is a debate that frequently comes up for air. Homosexuality, abortion and birth control are vexing topics.

In recent times, as everyone is aware, the scandals in the Roman Catholic Church have shaken that institution to its foundations. Bishops and priests are still being called out for practicing or harboring sexually deviant behavior and the substantial coffers of the Holy Mother Church have been strained.

Christians disagree on all manner of things, from the mundane to important articles of faith. Squabbles are common. However, as we've reiterated, man's imperfect practice of religion is tangential or irrelevant to the issue as to whether God exists and if so, whose side He is on, which may well be nobody's. There is no need for us to delve any further into these administrative matters, whether territorial or dogmatic. The salient problems with Christianity are spiritual.

One of the major characteristics of Christianity is the predominant role of guilt. Guilt and unworthiness have been the currency of Christianity since inception. In some cases, the analogy is literal: Martin Luther's instant reason to lead the Reformation was the selling of "indulgences" by the Roman Catholic church, allowing gain time in Purgatory.

The concept of original sin – that mankind is doomed without intervention because Adam and Eve ate an apple at the behest of a crafty snake – is the wellspring from which all else follows. It seems a fairy tale gone amok. Christians are born in sin, commit sin tirelessly, and basically have a negative worth. Eating the forbidden fruit introduced death into the world. This is despite the fact that Christianity believes man was created by God in His own image, and yet it took the sacrifice of God's son to restore man to the possibility of salvation.

In the case particularly of Roman Catholicism, it is noteworthy that few of the world's major religions have regarded its practitioners with such a violent lack of self-worth. It is to the great credit of Pope Francis that he has shined a positive light and begun to dispel the dark shadows of guilt and unworthiness cast across the faithful by centuries of an oppressive and often corrupt Roman infrastructure.

Because Christianity embraces both the New and Old Testaments, there is a problem of reconciliation between the two very different personalities of God as revealed in the scripture. The God of the Old Testament is vengeful, even conspiratorial, often petty, aiding ethnic or religious segments of society against others. The logic of this is difficult. Presumably God created all creatures, all races, all beings. Aiding one ethnic or religious group against another – the Jews against an unending series of other races, for example – seems bizarre, even trivial against the backdrop of our examination of the wondrous universe He created. The Great Flood, if it occurred, is a fearful act of genocide and has no relation to a loving God. One suspects these factional battles were inspired by man and that God did not pick sides.

Sometimes the underpinnings of an article of faith rest on a shaky foundation, as, for example, the Roman Catholic argument for Mary's Immaculate Conception.[44]

---

[44] Not to be confused with that of Jesus. This doctrine holds that Mary was born free of Original Sin, although likely conceived by normal means.

It is noteworthy that neither Mary nor Joseph claimed this to be the case, and neither did Jesus – in actuality, there is not a written word from any of them about anything at all. It was not until 1854 when Pope Pius IX affirmed the Mary's birth to be free from Original Sin that the concept was validated by the Roman Catholic Church, an affirmation largely at odds with the rest of Christianity. Regarding Jesus' lineage, Christianity is bound by the concept that Joseph was not Jesus' biological father, since John 1:14 states "And the Word became flesh, and dwelt among us." He was by definition a non-creation, having been an integral part of God forever. The claim of Mary's virginity is made by extension and argument, but does not seem theologically confirmed.

In any event, we know where these ideas came from. When claims of a Deity living on earth are made, those who believe often elevate his status by purifying his birth. This is pretty much a universal trait; there is ample precedent for claims of virgin births by religions around the world. Juno was impregnated by a flower; the god Mars was the result. The Mexican Queen of Heaven, Suchiquecal, conceived "without connection to a man." Yu, the Chinese emperor, was born of union between his mother and a star. Claims of Immaculate Conception extend to Chrishna (India) and Buddha. And so on.

Since in the case of Christ none of the principals themselves make the claim, and it was only belatedly affirmed in the nineteenth century, it becomes difficult to attach credence to the veracity of the virgin birth.

This doesn't stop the parade, however. The British Medical Journal reported a University of North Carolina birth study wherein .5% of respondents claim to have experienced a virgin birth.[45]

Documentation of the life of Christ as told in the gospels of Matthew, Mark, Luke and John is unclear, hardly surprising when given the age of the material and the inordinate period of time before anything was written down. Researchers do not fully agree on who wrote what and when, or even who these authors really were. Generally, it seems agreed that neither Luke nor Mark ever knew Jesus, so Christ's direct quotes from either of these apostles are hearsay twice removed and subject to interpretation and malleability over time. Claims the gospel of John is an eyewitness account are not completely accepted among scholars. It probably was written somewhere between A.D. 65 and 100, which would make the apostle John very old or dead. There is uncertainty as well as to which John is referred to in the gospels; there were several Johns in the life of Christ. There is also doubt as to whether Revelation was written by the same John, particularly because of the markedly different writing style

Generally, it is accepted that the first Gospel was penned around the year 70 by Mark; Luke and Matthew

---

[45] Christmas 2013: Strange Nativities, British Medical Journal, December 17, 2013

are derivative texts.   Together, they are considered
synoptic works.   The latter two, and perhaps John
(whose story differs appreciably from the others), are
believed to have had a second source for their writings,
dubbed "Q" by scholars[46].   In actuality, John's first
source is a question, particularly because of the date of
authorship.   The gospels are vague enough so that there
is debate as to whether Jesus had siblings or cousins, for
example[47]. This potentially complicates the claim by
some that Mary remained a virgin throughout her life.

　　　There is no clear explanation as to why those
scribes waited so long to write the gospels.   A claim is
that after the fall of Jerusalem in A.D. 70 the authors
feared the story would be lost, and thus decided to set it
all down in writing. Another theory is that Asian bishops
wished the story written down to counter heresy that
Jesus was not in existence before Mary.   Perhaps the
most logical is that these were oral times, with most
people illiterate, and the disciples were busy spreading
the word in person.

　　　Suffice to say it's all a bit cloudy, and as we've
noted not to be unexpected from ancient writings.   As
any detective will attest, cold case files are extremely
difficult to solve after a few years as memories become
fuzzy, witnesses die or disappear, evidence gets lost, etc.

---

[46] It is debatable whether Ian Fleming derived his "Q" from
Christian lore. Q, you will recall, supplied James Bond with his
deadly toys.
[47] Did Jesus Have Brothers and Sisters? Meghan Murphy-Gill, U.S.
Catholic, Vol. 78, No. 12, p. 46

It's really amazing to find as much material as there is, verifiable or not.

Crucifixion and ascendancy into Heaven are common themes in the years before Christ. Kersey Graves, in 1875, purported to document these in his book "The World's Sixteen Crucified Saviors". He identifies a similar number of holy ascendancies, many with similarities to Christ, including, oddly enough, common December 25 birthdates[48]. Material from this book has been quoted in later works repudiating the validity of Christ, although Graves' book has been criticized but apparently never fully repudiated.

While Christ's life is not fully documented, the years between ages 12 and 30 are particularly blank. While this proves nothing, it seems particularly odd for someone who is God/Man, especially if he was toiling away as a carpenter and whose higher purpose was dormant for almost two decades. The immediate events after his death are likewise a mystery. Where he went for three days (if indeed he did) after dying on the cross is the subject of conjecture. One story, described in Acts 2:24-28 and preserved in The Apostles Creed, has it that he descended into Hell for a time. This is by no means a universal Christian view, however. Opinions are all over the lot. Some say – primarily Roman Catholics - he went into Limbo[49], a special place for the souls of unbaptized

[48] In Jesus' case, the December 25 date is probably arbitrary. There is no agreement among scholars as to the actual date.
[49] Limbo is no longer officially recognized by the R.C. church.

infants and deserving souls who predeceased Christ. While there, he is said to have released these folks who would now be able to ascend into Heaven, since he had just retroactively paid for their sins on the cross. This prayer also proclaims that Jesus ascended into Heaven after three days; however, this claim is repudiated by Christ's own words when he told one of the thieves on the cross next to him that he would join him in Paradise that very day. Some theologians, troubled by this apparent discrepancy, have attempted to interpret Christ's utterance as not really meaning the same day. The tortured logic that arrives at this conclusion is an interesting study of man's ability to rationalize almost anything.

One of the most troubling difficulties is the failure of those who knew Jesus best to recognize him after his resurrection, as described by Luke and John. This includes Mary Magdalene as well as the apostles. Reading the strained and contrived explanations by authorities and proponents of Christianity as to why Jesus was not known are not comforting to those seeking the truth. The concept smacks of collusion and deception. If Christ was indeed divine, why would he let that happen?

Another of the complexities of Christianity is reconciliation with the statements attributed to Jesus stating that heaven is only attainable through him. John 14:6 quotes Jesus: "I am the way, the truth, and the life: no man cometh unto the Father but by me." So what about those who predated Christ? Did Jesus truly descend into Hell – or Limbo - and lead those deserving souls to salvation? And, if so, does this validate the theories of works or grace? In theory, those souls got to Limbo or wherever because of their good works, but are then saved by grace – Jesus' rescue.

Attempts to deal with the eventual fate of those who predated Christ, as well as heathen cultures and civilizations where Christ is unknown, are equivocal. Most attempts to explain this are fuzzy, stating the Lord is a loving God and will take care of these people somehow. Implicit in this position, though, is the ignoring of the petulant, often lethal acts attributed to God in the Old Testament. The preposition is often changed to God "of" the Old Testament, which is interesting and conciliatory to the contrasting nature attributed to Him before Christ.

This leads to the overall debate as to how heaven is attained: through faith alone, works, or some combination of the two. This is a key problem that has been a thorn in the side of Christianity since Christ's lifetime. Roman Catholics believe the deceased must be in a state of grace to attain heaven. This state is attained by confession of sins and subsequent absolution, a view not shared by other sects. The Bible itself scatters explanations all over the lot, and they don't always agree.

James, for instance, writes three times that faith without works is dead. While these statements are plainly written, those who proclaim faith alone is the gateway to heaven proffer tortured explanations in attempting to repudiate them. Jesus himself in several places denies salvation to the sinner. Matthew 19:16-26:

"And behold, a man came up to him, saying, "Teacher, what good deed must I do to have eternal life?" And he said to him, "Why do you ask me what is good? There is only one who is good. If you would enter life, keep the commandments.""

Indeed, of what use are the commandments if they carry no weight?

Jesus addresses the question again in John 5:28-29:

"Marvel not at this: for the hour is coming, when all who are in the graves shall hear his voice, And shall come forth; they that have done good, unto the resurrection of life; and they that have done evil, unto the resurrection of damnation."

Seem plain enough? This seems to settle the question of retroactive absolution.

And this quote from Jesus as described in Matthew 19:25:

"Again I say to you, it is easier for a camel to go through the eye of a needle, than for a rich man to enter the kingdom of God."

Remember too that Matthew is generally believed to have known Jesus; he indeed was the tax collector referenced by Christ. His quote is first person hearsay, while John's quotations from Jesus may not be.

The apostle Paul takes the opposite view, indicating grace is the key ingredient to a heavenly reward. Disagreement on this point is endless and still rages; the dispute was a key to the Reformation and founding of Protestantism by Martin Luther. While the reasons for the schism are complex, the inciting incident is generally agreed as Luther's objection to the selling of indulgences – gain time for Heaven – by the church.

There are those who argue that if one is a true believer in Christ, he will thus do good works. These may be the same bunch who denies the fossil record. This argument is not worth the ink to refute, whether it's the Crusades, Salem witch trials, predator priests, bad Popes or virtually all of mankind. The only believer in Christ who consistently did good works was Christ himself, and maybe Mother Teresa and a few others we don't know about.

Doubtless, though, the most vexing problem for followers of Christ is his apparently whopping error when he predicted his own return before the current generation would have passed on[50]. There are tens of thousands of words written by defenders of Christ in what appear agonized attempts to explain this away. Even such a staunch defender of the faith as C.S. Lewis has trouble:

---

[50] Matthew 24:34, Mark 13:1-37, Luke 21:5-33. These are collectively known as the Olivet Discourse.

"Say what you like," we shall be told [by some critics], "the apocalyptic beliefs of the first Christians have been proved to be false. It is clear from the New Testament that they all expected the Second Coming in their own lifetime. And, worse still, they had a reason, and one which you will find very embarrassing. Their Master had told them so. He shared, and indeed created, their delusion. He said in so many words, 'This generation shall not pass till all these things be done.' And he was wrong. He clearly knew no more about the end of the world than anyone else." [Here the imaginary critics end speaking. CS Lewis begins next.]

> It is certainly the most embarrassing verse in the Bible. Yet how teasing, also, that within fourteen words of it should come the statement "But of that day and that hour knoweth no man, no, not the angels which are in heaven, neither the Son, but the Father." The one exhibition of error and the one confession of ignorance grow side by side."[51]

Even more explicit, we find in Matthew 16:27,28:
"For the son of Man is going to come in the glory of his Father with His angels, and will then repay every man according to his deeds. Truly I say to you, there are some of those who are standing here who will not taste

---

[51] The Essential C.S. Lewis, p. 385, "The World's Last Night" essay

death until they see the Son of Man coming in His Kingdom."

Not only does Christ come down squarely on the side (again) of the necessity of doing good works to attain salvation[52], he predicts his own triumphant return before the death of everyone in the crowd.

This did not happen.

Christian detractors also point to Christ's last words, variously translated as "My God, my God, why hast thou forsaken me?"[53]

It is important to remember that Christian doctrine holds that Christ was part man. This would have included the ability to feel pain, without which the sacrifice on the cross would have been meaningless. At that point, Jesus had been on the cross for hours. He'd been whipped, scourged and pierced with a spear. To hold his last words up as a refutation of his credentials is a failing and cruel argument. In one light it may be seen as an affirmation, at least of Christ's own belief in the Father.

* * * *

We need to balance this chapter by noting that an incredible number of good works are performed throughout the world in the name of Christianity, whether the faith is true or not. It is overall a positive

---

[52] Why the faith v works argument persists seems a denial of logic.
[53] Matthew 27:46

and uplifting force. As we've pointed out, though, there are troubling difficulties with the dogma.

When one takes a step back to gain perspective, it almost appears as if Christianity has succeeded (up until now) in spite of serious theological difficulties. We can conclude that man desperately wants to believe in something higher and better and will overlook what seem like critical flaws to do so.

Chapter 17 **God in Prime Time**

Nowhere in America is the quest for God more active than in the phenomenon and propagation of Christian megachurches. Megachurches commonly share several characteristics:[54]

- 2,000 or more persons in weekly attendance
- A charismatic, authoritative senior minister
- A very active, 7 day a week congregational community
- A multitude of social and outreach ministries
- A complex differentiated organizational structure

A forerunner to the megachurch, at least as far as weekly audience and a charismatic preacher is concerned, would be Bishop Fulton J. Sheen's ministry. The Catholic cleric's *Life is Worth Living* television show ran during the 1950s and continued through the 1960s as *The Fulton Sheen Program*. Getting his media

---

[54] Hartford Institute for Religious Research

start in 1930, Sheen's radio broadcasts ran for twenty years before he moved to the tube.

Sheen was a true theologian, winning the Cardinal Mercier Prize for International Philosophy in 1923, and teaching at the Catholic University of America. A mesmerizing preacher with impeccable credentials, Sheen's many accomplishments included the authorship of an astounding 73 books. His uncompromising morality eventually cost him his job, refusing to bow to Cardinal Spellman's attempt to extort millions of dollars for powdered milk donated by the federal government. Sheen did not equivocate or mince words and was successful anyway. He was one of a kind, as the nature of televangelism changed after him and not for the better. A movement to canonize Archbishop Sheen, begun in 2002, did not come to fruition.

Much of the success of subsequent televangelists and megachurches can be attributed to two things: powerful use of the media and a positive message, usually emphasizing personal growth and success on earth. On the flip side, the chicanery of faith healing continues as a staple moneymaker, keeping whole networks afloat as well as the healers' banks accounts. From tent to tube, the showbiz stage tricks of the quack healers haven't changed much in a hundred years.

The 1992 Steve Martin film *Leap of Faith* is an entertaining and revealing work[55] about the subject, as is the classic *Elmer Gantry*, for which Burt Lancaster won the Academy Award for Best Actor.   Perhaps the most ludicrous example of today's faith healers, Benny Hinn, evidently couldn't cure himself as he was hospitalized in March 2015 suffering from atrial fibrillation.

The roots of the megachurch phenomenon can be traced back to preachers such as California's Rev. Robert Schuller.   Schuller began preaching at a drive-in movie in 1955 with the catch slogan "Worship as you are in the family car".   And they did.   Schuller's Garden Grove Community Church flourished.   After inviting Dr. Norman Vincent Peale to speak, Schuller came to a realization. Introduced to salesmanship through Peale, he saw that extolling the personal benefits of Christianity was a positive and powerful attraction, much more so than chastising his audience for their sins.   He adapted his sermons, and the ministry mushroomed.   His popular television show, *The Hour of Power*, successfully culminated in the building of the Crystal Cathedral in Orange County.   Unfortunately, the place wound up deeply in debt after Schuller retired.   There were succession problems – Schuller fired his son Robert as senior pastor - and bankruptcy resulted.   As delineated above, the personality of the megachurch preacher is a powerful magnetic force and when that force is lost the

---

[55] "Real miracles, sensibly priced."

organization often disintegrates. The preacher with the charismatic appeal has become the surrogate for God.

Billy Graham has represented the conservative Protestant mainstream throughout his long history of broadcasts, sermons, rallies and revivals. Much admired, Graham has spoken out repeatedly against the fractionalized sects and denominations of Protestantism. Known for his association with the elite and powerful, he has been the spiritual advisor to many American presidents, a job he failed totally where Richard Nixon was concerned.[56] Graham has been dubbed the Chaplain of the White House. He has always been one of America's most admired people.

Subsequent preachers have not always been as well grounded in the spiritual as Billy Graham. The television ministry business was quick to realize that earthly rewards prove a much more attractive audience draw than sin. Commercial religion took a bizarre turn, completely outside the teachings of Christ. Elmer Gantry was out, Joel Osteen in. It remains there today.

The rise of Protestant megachurches, largely at the expense of traditional Christian sects such as Methodist and Presbyterian, is an American phenomenon. The largest of these is Joel Osteen's Lakewood Church in Houston.

The Lakewood Church operation represents a grotesque extension from the roots of evangelical media pioneered by Bishop Sheen and Billy Graham. Robert

---

[56] Understandable, considering the material he had to work with.

Schuller's operation can perhaps be viewed as a bridge between the old and the new. Osteen is a multimillionaire. He is the "prosperity preacher", heading the biggest of the megachurches. The cornerstone of Osteen's ministry is reward on earth. No cross appears onstage, Biblical references are few, and Jesus plays a minor role. Author of many books, a typical Osteen title that sums up the ministry is "Your Best Life Now". A miniature Tony Robbins, Osteen appears as a goggle-eyed puppy dog, with a sappy smile that can turn to tears in an instant when questioned by skeptical reporters, as occurred on **Sixty Minutes**.

Roots of organizations like Osteen's can be traced to the Christian oppressive views grounded in sin and punishment, as explored earlier. American youth, in particular, no longer accept the Puritanical and debilitating doctrines that man is born of sin and continues to sin, unworthy in the sight of God. They rejoice instead of repent, beat drums to upbeat music instead of beating their chests and wailing to solemn hymns. It is the times.

The proliferation of television channels, some religious, has aided in the expansion of all sorts of fringe preachers, faith healers, and bizarre personalities. The fact that even the most grotesque of these can gather a following who pay for the air time and extravagant lifestyles with donations speaks to the sophistication and gullibility of the audiences. When one falls, it's usually spectacular. It seems to make little difference though as, like bloated corpses, the same disgraced God peddlers usually bob to the surface again.

Here's a short list of all-star fallen televangelists:[57]

Bob Coy, founder of Calvary Chapel, which became Florida's largest megachurch of 20,000 members, was guilty of a number of affairs and an admitted compulsive porn watcher.

Jimmy Swaggert, southern hellfire TV preacher and cousin to rock 'n' roll legend Jerry Lee Lewis, was nailed with prostitutes in 1986 and 1991, and supposedly was interested on one's thirteen year old daughter.[58] He's back on TV along with his relatives.

Ted Haggard, founder of New Life Church in Colorado, was caught in a homosexual affair and was accused of being a crystal meth user. Haggard was the subject of an HBO special chronicling his fall from grace and subsequent fruitless attempts to gain employment.

Louis Lamonica, pastor of Hosanna Church in Louisiana, confessed to animal sacrifice and child abuse by himself and his parishioners. Supposedly he was the inspiration for the *True Detective* TV hit series starring Woody Harrelson and Matthew McConaughey.

Isaac Hunter, former megachurch pastor, committed suicide after being exposed having an affair with a church member. His wife had been granted a

---

[57] International Business Times, UK, April 13, 2014
[58] It seems to run in the family.

restraining order because of erratic behavior and left her "fearing for my life and the lives of our three children".

Jim Bakker, televangelist and co-host of the Christian PTL Club, was accused of rape and went to prison for embezzlement. After six years in the slammer, Jim is back on TV.

Many others have been accused of financial malfeasance. Paul and Jan Crouch[59], who founded the Trinity Broadcasting Network, were accused of defrauding $50 million from the network. The money in the televangelism game is astonishing, and it attracts the worst of mankind. It also shows a percentage of people will follow anything, no matter how bizarre, corrupt or obvious, and that is an important point to keep in mind when considering man's attempts to connect with the Almighty.

---

[59] The name may be unfamiliar but you know Jan - the woman with the gigantic cotton candy pink wig, fake eyelashes and a pound of mascara.

Chapter 18   Israel and Judaism: A Religious Rubik's Cube

Jews believe they are the Chosen People, but chosen for what? The history of the Jewish people throughout history has largely been one of oppression and hardship, persecution and scorn. Out of the ashes of the Holocaust the nation of Israel arose and has flourished, and perhaps that is the evidence for belief, but it is a short moment in a long history of dismal occurrences.

The theme of being God's elite has its roots in the Torah, the five Old Testament books commonly held as having been written by Moses, and continues throughout other Jewish writings. These books are Genesis, Exodus, Leviticus, Numbers and Deuteronomy. An example is found in Deuteronomy 7:6, "The Lord your God has chosen you to be His treasured people, out of all the peoples upon the face of the earth." Of course, if this was really written by Moses, his view wasn't exactly unbiased.

The idea of a God who creates everybody and then picks favorites is seen by non-Jews as ethnic elitism, if not downright nonsensical, and obviously this concept has not borne much earthly fruit. However, although rabbinical scholars differ on the nature of an afterlife, if any, there is a theme of Jewish heaven being a bit better than non-Jewish paradise, as we will see below.

Judaism is a relatively minor religion, with only fourteen million members worldwide. There are twice as many Sikhs, for example, yet Judaism is generally classified as a major religion whereas Sikhism is not. Dr. Adam Gregerman postulates that the prominence given to Judaism is because of its common roots with Christianity and Islam.   In America, he continues, Judaism has always received an elevated amount of publicity and a sort of co-equal status with Christianity in American literature when the term Judeo-Christian society came into use. The term appeared in a 1963 Supreme Court case.[60]

Be that as it may, Judaism is a curious religion for several reasons. One of the biggest is the doctrine on Heaven and Hell.

There isn't any.

Or, more correctly, there are perhaps too many. The Talmud, for instance, describes Gan Eden, or Olam HaBa, the next world. Gehennom is a hell of intense punishment and cleansing. But this is just a springboard; Jewish scholars have written diversely of the afterlife – if any.

---

[60] Institute for Christian & Jewish Studies, ICSJS.org, 2014, Is Judaism a Major World Religion?

The Pirke Evot (Ethics of the Fathers) says earth is "the corridor where one prepares himself to enter the banquet hall" by obeying the commandments. Orthodox Rabbi Eliezer Finkelman figures the maximum a soul spends in Gehennom is eleven months.[61] By that time the soul is cleansed enough to move on, presumably to Olam HaBa. Finkelman's mathematical reasoning and computations are interesting, if obscure. This is, as one might imagine, not a universal Jewish view.

There are incredibly detailed and fanciful descriptions of punishment. There is, some believe, a Gehennom-of-Snow which is apt punishment for those who exhibited a coldness towards the Torah. As one might guess, there is a Gehennom-of-Fire, which is sixty times (60) hotter than earthly fire. This place is reserved for those who had a passion for forbidden activities. Since the average paper fire is 1500 degrees F or so, the Gehennom-of-Fire clocks in at a really hot 90,000 degrees F, or about nine times the surface temperature of the sun. It seems a big price to pay for fooling around with the secretary.

Some scholars such as Rosenblatt Feld say Jews are favored in Olam HaBa because they were mistreated in this world. What happens to those inhabitants of wealthy Jewish enclaves such as in Palm Beach[62] or on Long Island is unexplained, but, as one might imagine, this is a popular view.

---

[61] Which is why Kaddish lasts eleven months less one day
[62] Many of these Jews were mistreated by Bernie Madoff, though.

There are also provisions for reincarnation, which might surprise a significant number of Jews. According to the Kabbalah (a collection of texts discussing Jewish mystical tradition) Jewish souls keep coming back until 613 commandments have been performed.[63] That certainly seems like a lot, but most are passive negatives. The list of these commandments, commonly known as the Law of Moses, is somewhat described in the Talmud. Of these, 365 are negative commandments, and correspond to the days of the year, while the remaining 248 are positive, and correlate with the number of bones and main organs in the human body.[64] Why is a separate and unanswered question.

Reb Chaim Vital championed the idea that there are several different types of souls. Some are pure, some have the good qualities of other souls, some the bad, others are loaners, having once belonged to another person.[65] The number of times a soul can recycle is not specified.

Just to stir the mix, some Jews believe souls keep moving higher and higher towards G-d (nothing much happens if you spell it out), cleansing and freeing themselves from earthly spoils. Just how they move higher is not always clear, especially if limited to eleven months in Gehennom. Rabbi Tzvi Freeman is convinced

---

[63] Jewish Views on the Afterlife, Lisa Klug, Interfaith Family, April 1999
[64] Jewish Virtual Library
[65] Shalar HaGigulim/The Gate of Transmigration of Souls, Reb Chaim Vital

the souls will be united with physical bodies in this
world, although which bodies and what state they will be
in is likewise unclear.[66]

The seemingly unending list of Jewish rituals and
practices are way too long, arcane, complex, detailed,
diverse, sectionally fractured and mundane to describe
here. They are rich in tradition, meaning, triviality and
obscurity. Many seem completely nutty, a characteristic
shared by rituals of many other faiths. As we said at the
outset, to lose ourselves in the details of particular
religions is contrary to our overarching purpose. A broad
brush is enough to give us perspective.

An interesting and entertaining Coen Brothers
film, *A Serious Man* (Focus Features, 2009), depicts
many of the Jewish traditions in a comedic light and is a
worthwhile experience.

It is interesting to note that in recent years
Judaism has been moving toward the more conservative
and Orthodox practice.[67] A chafing point, though, is the
derogatory treatment of women, one that is not likely to
be relieved to any real degree. This is perhaps a bigger
problem in Israel than in the United States.

Judaism's lack of unanimity regarding the
spiritual and the emphasis on earthly ritual is not a
criticism per se. As noted before, in the end nothing can

---

[66] Bringing Heaven Down to Earth, Rabbi Tzvi Freeman, senior
editor Chabad.org
[67] Michael Kress, Orthodox Judaism: The State of Orthodox Judaism
Today, Jewish Virtual Library Online

be proved or disproved, only intelligently surmised, and that may not be enough.

Putting it another way, and to misquote screenwriter William Goldman about the movie business and the ability to predict a hit, "Nobody knows nuttin'."

*　　　*　　　*　　　*　　　*

In the world today, Israel has been held as a shining triumph, a concrete example of man's ability to rise from hardship and persecution, to persevere and overcome incredible odds. And this is so, but it is a double-sided coin. Israel is also an example of mankind's darkest side.

One of the most discouraging occurrences in modern history is that nation's treatment of Palestinians over the years since the creation of Israel. The Palestinian Diaspora is not without irony; Israeli persecution and banishment of Palestinians from their homeland is well-documented and difficult to deny[68]. Palestinians' determination to return to a land that 97% of them have never seen continues to stoke the furnace of unrest and this continual activity is partially responsible for a backlash against Israel. The fires of persecution still burn, it seems, while the ashes of the Holocaust are still warm.

Of all the human traits, perhaps the most predictable is man's inhumanity to man.

---

[68] "Palestine Refugees: 50 Years of Injustice", The Permanent Observer Mission of Palestine to the United Nations, Nov 28, 2002

Chapter 19 – The Resurgence of Radicalism and Ultra-Orthodoxy

This right-wing trend mentioned in the last chapter is not confined in America to Judaism – evangelical Christianity, Mormonism and other sects can be seen as a reaction to an increasingly left-leaning and permissive American society. These trends, as well as the increasing population segments espousing them, are aided by the prolific reproductive nature of these groups. Included among them are the Amish, Mennonite and similar sects. Many tend to be reclusive, keeping to their own and shunning much of the American mainstream and its permissive social mores.

Abroad, of course, the situation is far worse. Much of the world has retreated into a state of barbarism not known for hundreds of years. The rise of ISIS, groups like al Qaeda and the resurgence of medieval Sharia Law are seen both a reaction against mainstream Islam as well as a counterrevolution against the spread of secularism, particularly as championed by the west. Attempts to marginalize these radical practices and beliefs have been met with furious, and often violent, resistance.[69] This has all been exacerbated by the Arab Spring, which has thus far proven pretty much a dud after an impressive start. Today, the west and moderate Arab states are at war with these forces around the world and face terrorist activities everywhere. The religious and quasi-religious backlash against secularism and permissiveness is not limited to Middle Eastern Arab countries.   Reactive movements in Israel, India and Algeria have mirrored this phenomenon.

The Western world is seemingly at a loss as how to deal with these radicals, who exhibit a level of barbarism not seen since the Middle Ages.   In some ways, the phenomenon is a self-fulfilling prophecy, the culmination of unending meddling into the Middle East by the West for well over a century, largely motivated by greed to acquire the region's oil. Echoes of Genesis 1:27 only make one shake his head and form a wry smile: "So God created mankind in his own image…"

As of now, guns, tanks, drones and bombs are the only answer that has been effective to any degree. These may always be the only answer.

---

[69] The Paradox of Liberation: Secular Revolutions and Religious Counterrevolutions, Michael Walzer, Yale University Press, March 2015

Chapter 20 – The Bible: Suspension of Disbelief

We have referred to a number of Biblical stories and descriptions throughout as evidence of the inadvisability of taking that work literally. This is especially relevant since so many of the world's religions base their faiths, in whole or in part, on the Old Testament and others on the entire anthology. Before moving past our brief overview of organized religion, we are obliged to strengthen this position because it has deeper ramifications.

It is very easy to take potshots at the Bible and I stress the fact that it is not the intent to discredit the book completely, but rather to show as concretely as possible that the book is not a literal work. There are implications beyond the simple stories and fables because Jesus Christ has endorsed (for want of a better word) Biblical tales which to any reasonable person would have no possibility of having occurred. Two of these instances follow:

Stories of The Great Flood, or a great flood, are found in the lore of many faiths and civilizations. Documents go back as far as 4,000 plus years to describe a great flood in the Fertile Crescent that destroyed civilization, save for a single family who built a giant boat.[70] Stories of the event, or others similar to it, are found all over the world. The cataclysmic event is described in the Old Testament and is a marker for Christian and Jewish faiths.

Perhaps no example of the suspension of disbelief described earlier is more apt that the story of Noah and the flood, on many levels. Placidly accepting the concept that God would kill everyone and everything by drowning, saving only eight people and a representative sample of animals, is normally beyond rational acceptance. The reason for this mass genocide appears to be God's displeasure with man, his creation. Mankind had degenerated into lawlessness and sin, we are advised, except for Noah and his family whose bloodline was pure. This grieved God greatly.[71] He said to Noah:

"Go into the ark, you and all your household, for I have seen that you are righteous before me in this generation. Take with you seven pairs of all clean animals, the male and his mate, and a pair of animals that are not clean, the male and his mate, and seven pairs of the birds of the heavens also, male and female, to keep their offspring alive on the face of the earth."

There is actually dispute among those so interested as to the exact language; the translation may be seven individual specimens or seven pair. The fact than an odd number was specified leads to the supposition that

---

[70] Jewish History.org & The Destiny Foundation
[71] Genesis 6

God meant pairs, or perhaps more accurately the writer meant pairs, but against the backdrop of the whole affair who knows?

There is no guidance in these passages as to what constituted clean animals as opposed to unclean ones. Pigeons might be classified as unclean, seeing what they've done to our cities. One can only guess why seven pair (or just seven) of certain unspecified species were to be rounded up and put aboard. God gave Noah and his family of eight somewhere south of a hundred years to build this temporary seaworthy zoo, acquire and store food, gather the animals, capture the birds. Since Noah lived to be about 950, this didn't put too big a dent in his lifestyle. After that, rain fell for forty days and nights. Everyone and everything was wiped out, including babies and young children, innocents swept up in the flood tide of God's wrath.

No rational person can give a moment's credence to this fable, yet Christians, Jews and a number of other sects believe the story, including the tale that Noah had three sons after attaining the age of 500, a mean feat at one tenth the years. Again, if God exists, He can do anything, and that would include helping Noah build the floating zoo and stock it as well as killing everyone and everything in sight. Barring his assistance, though, even the most cursory examination finds the Flood a logistical impossibility.

One thing of note that makes this tale of singular importance - Jesus gave credence to the Flood story:[72]

"They ate, they drank, they married wives; they were given in marriage, until the day when Noah entered the ark, and the flood came and destroyed them all."

Now this is a very interesting quote for many reasons. It is third person hearsay at best, since Luke never met Jesus, but he seems to have gotten the story and quotation from Paul. We can make several observations:

1. Jesus may never have said it.
2. He may have been misquoted.
3. If Jesus did say it as written, it indicates he knew about the event, which implies either a historical record or divine knowledge.
4. It gives some weight to the story.
5. There appears to be no sinful activity in the actions Jesus ascribes to pre-Flood man. He seems to have been referencing the everyday, apparently for dramatic effect.
6. If Jesus was truly divine, then the Flood actually happened because he said it did.

There are strong and powerful forces at work for intelligent people to give credence to the story of the Flood. Not the least is the morality of disbelief as described in this chapter.

---

[72] Luke 17:27

One of the more grotesque reasons offered for the event is postulated by Austin Robbins, DD, from the Association for Biblical Research.   Dr. Robbins is convinced the seed of sinful angels had infected the human bloodline as a result of angel/human fornication, contaminating all except for Noah and his family. This was part of Satan's plot to prevent a sinless Savior from being born.[73] God thwarted the plan by killing everyone and starting over (the animals are unexplained).

I'm not kidding, this seemingly educated individual actually said that.

There is little one can add to the above, except to conclude the idea is completely batty, and perhaps to note that Hollywood seems to have lifted the concept for the recent spate of vampire films. Actually, the film industry has found this a popular subject for many years. The Omen films and Rosemary's Baby are examples.

A second Biblical event we are obliged to examine is the story of Jonah and the whale, or giant fish. Jonah had failed to do God's bidding and preach to the people of Nineveh, whom had evidently fallen quite heavily into sin.[74] This displeased God, and the result is described in Jonah 1:17.

"Now the Lord had prepared a great fish to swallow up Jonah. And Jonah was in the belly of the fish three days and three nights."

---

[73] Why Did God Send the Flood? Associates for Biblical Research, June 28, 2006

[74] This happens a lot in the Old Testament. People haven't changed.

And then:

"And the Lord spake unto the fish, and it vomited out Jonah upon the dry land."

A rational person would likely consider the tale whimsy or allegory at best, and move on to more contemplative matters. However, this fish tale is, like the Great Flood, referred to specifically by Jesus Christ, putting the story in another category altogether:

"For as Jonah was three days and three nights in the whale's belly, so shall the Son of man be three days and three nights in the heart of the earth."[75]

It isn't a stretch to say that the lynchpin of Christianity, the divinity of Jesus Christ, is on the line by his endorsement of these two Biblical events as factual. Additionally, this quote is at odds with Christ's words on the cross, indicating the thief next to him would join Jesus in Paradise that very day. At best, somebody is misquoting Christ. The alternative is more troubling.

It gives pause.

Yes, if God exists He can say or do whatever He likes, as we've pointed out on several occasions, including a massive Do-Over in the case of Noah and putting someone into a fish for several days as a novel punishment. But is it likely? Do these two Biblical stories lend themselves more to Walt Disney than God?

Again, it gives pause.

---

[75] Matthew 12:40

Another difficulty with the Bible is that it seems to admit God makes mistakes while claiming he doesn't. Genesis 6:6-7:

"And it repented the Lord that he had made man on the earth, and it grieved him at his heart. And the Lord said, I will destroy man whom I have created from the face of the earth; both man, and beast, and the creeping thing, and the fowls of the air; for it repenteth me that I have made them."

That is *really* being annoyed at a mistake.

He also changes His mind (Jonah 3:10), and apparently doesn't always know the future:

"When God saw what they did, how they turned from their evil way, God relented of the disaster that He had said He would do to them, and He did not do it."

The folks of Nineveh dodged a bullet. And again, in Exodus 32:14, when God caught the Israelites worshipping a golden calf:

"And the Lord relented from the disaster that He had spoken of bringing on his people."

We can go on and on, but the point is made. It doesn't need to be hammered, does it?

And again, as stressed often throughout this book, none of this means or proves there is a God or no God. All it does is illustrate what is believed is often beyond reason. To hold the Bible up as proof or denial of God is an error. It is a book. So is the Qur'an, the Vedas, the Torah, the Pyramid Texts, the Diamond Sutra, the Guru

Granth Sahib, the Bhagavad Gita, the sutras, Chairman Mao's Little Red Book, and on and on.

It is no easy task to lift the fog of "Sunday thinking" and afford a clearer view of the emotional component of the problem.

Chapter 21 Religion Custom Fit

Religion will shape itself to fit the cultural and economic mores of the group espousing it. In the United States, white Anglo-Saxons have traditionally enjoyed the greatest prosperity and social acceptance of any ethnic division, and their religion has reflected this. The white Protestantism ethos of the twentieth century embraced moderation, genteelism, elitism, and a gentle tolerance of mild sin. God is good to his people, and often rewards them ahead of schedule. This mind-set has shifted even further with the proliferation of megachurches, which, as we have seen, have gradually leaned toward the secular, stressing earthly rewards and social conviviality over dogma and stern morality.

In Puritan times, life was hard. People died early, winter seemed endless, crops sometimes failed. Religion was hard as well. Punishment on earth was a component of the faith. While burning of witches was a horrendous aberration, the practice revealed an intolerance reflected in the living conditions of those times in New England and elsewhere. Suffering meant identifying with the essence of Christianity: Christ's travail on the cross.

And obviously some people needed to be blamed.

Roman Catholicism during the latter half of the twentieth century moved a bit toward inclusion and acknowledgement of the church's faithful, a novel concept at the time. The R.C. church began to recognize needs to a degree, only less so than Protestantism, being more rigidly bound by doctrine and hindered by a wealthy and cumbersome hierarchy. This more authoritative brand of Christianity was better suited to the ethnicity of many of its constituents, especially in Latin and South America.

The lax moral standards in America have increasingly spurred reaction among religious groups. Judaism has undergone interesting changes, having withdrawn into itself in many areas. The resurgence of Orthodoxy, as we have noted, is a reaction. This is mirrored in sects like the Amish, Mennonites and the like. Since 1960, for example, the Amish population of Lancaster County, Pennsylvania has almost tripled.[76] Overall, the Amish population has exploded from 5,000 in 1920 to 84,000 in 1984 and 300,000 today.[77]

America is not what it was, and neither is American religion.

Black America, which in 1990 was half Baptist, has diversified little in the ensuing years, although Baptists still claim 45% of the population. 87% of blacks are affiliated with a religion, four percentage points higher than Americans in general. Interestingly,

---

[76] LancasterPA.com, 2015
[77] USA Today, Matthew Diebel, August 16, 2014

somewhere between 15% and 30% of blacks were Muslim when imported as slaves, but they have converted primarily to Baptist with some becoming Catholic, primarily in Louisiana[78].

While blacks have made apparent strides toward social equality, the progress has largely been illusory, confined mostly to film, television[79], music, a few visible public positions as well as Barack Obama and his appointees. The economics of the black populace remains dismal, and thus religion remains a strong component of black life.

Since nine eleven, the specter of Muslim terrorism has cast a shadow over the world. Religious practices, martyrdom, intricacies of faiths and sects are a rabbit's warren we shall not delve into. Suffice to say there are madmen of every faith; fanaticism increases exponentially with deprivation and persecution. The only observation salient to our purposes here is that on balance these activities tend to lead one to a conclusion that if God exists, he is absent, at least from the Middle East.

---

[78] BlackDemographics.com: The Black Church
[79] Pioneered by MTV

Chapter 22 The Psychology of Belief

The daughter of a friend had graduated high school. She was the prom queen and also voted Most Likely. Extremely bright and insightful, she went off the rails not long thereafter. The young woman dropped out of college and was hospitalized for anorexia two or three times. Her health was in great jeopardy. After a lengthy stay in a sort of food rehab place, I asked her about it.

"What goes on in your mind about food?" I asked. "Why won't you eat? Why do you purge your stomach? Do you realize you've gone off the rails?"

As I said, she is a very intelligent person with a great sense of humor, so I knew I could get away with the question.

"You don't understand," she replied. I was saddened to see how haggard she looked, ten years older.

"Boy, are you right. Enlighten me."

"Look, here's the thing. An alcoholic knows that if he takes one drink, he's opened the floodgates and he's probably going to go on a jag and wind up in the hospital or worse, right?"

I followed that. "Sure."

"Well, it's the same thing. I'm afraid that if I take one bite of steak or cake or asparagus I won't be able to stop and I'll wind up really fat."

I could sort of understand the part about the cake, if it was chocolate.

"Yeah, but you've never been fat."

"Of course I have. I'm fat now. Look at me!"

"What do you see in the mirror?" She was alarmingly thin, almost like the poster people from concentration camps.

"I'm fat."

"But of course you're not fat! You're skin and bones."

"So you say." She plucked a hanging fold of loose skin. I cringed. "See?"

An anorexic sees fat where none exists, purges in the bathroom. A fat person looks in the mirror and sees someone fit, eats another doughnut. We see what we want to see.

Most of us want to be right with God. We may not be sure He is really there, but we hope He is and that He loves us. After all, don't many religions preach that God loves us, especially since Christ changed everything? If we're Christian, we have that comfort: Jesus said so. To doubt, then, is perilous to our well-being. Down deep, though, we may find articles of our faiths that seem silly, wrong, outmoded. Things are unproven, often contradictory. We push these feelings away because we feel a vague guilt to even have thought them.   Faith becomes subverted to mean we should believe in something that doesn't seem right, a tenet that can't be proven, a matter of conjecture taken as fact.   To question is to abandon faith.   Abandoned faith implies failure, disappointment to others, treason of a sort.

A deranged leader, convinced he is the messiah, tells his flock to kill themselves and their children and they do so without question.   How do cults of death led by people like David Koresh and Jim Jones come to power?   How do they override the instinct for self-preservation, to protect their young?

Charles Manson had but a handful of followers; aberrations like helter skelter are thus more understandable.   A few people can be swayed to do anything, pretty much.   In a supposedly enlightened country, though, how do madmen like Warren Jeffs or Ron Hubbard gain so many followers?

And how do we graduate to a whole other league, when entire nations are involved?   Joseph Stalin, Adolf Hitler, Pol Pot?   Idi Amin, Mao Zedong, Muammar Gaddafi?   And on and on - the list is near endless.

We have to recognize that the human psyche is capable of unlimited self-deception.   We are especially vulnerable when our cerebrum tells us an article of faith seems wrong but our cerebellum wants to believe it.   We laugh at the faith healer but send him money and limp into his tent to be cured, if only figuratively.   The state preys on this trait, raking in hundreds of millions in lottery money, often from people on food stamps or welfare.

Societies can turn to madness with frightening ease. They can be as schools of fish which dart and turn in an instant, seemingly as one. Any country is three meals away from revolution. Man's capacity for cruelty is boundless, the bottom side of the human coin. Since the twentieth century alone, mass acts of genocide include the following:[80]

Armenia – 1915-1923. Ottoman Empire massacres over one million ethnic Armenians, Assyrians and Greeks

Holocaust – 1933-1945. Nazi Germany slaughters six million Jews, five million Slavs, dissidents, Jehovah's Witnesses, disabled, mentally defective.

Cambodia – 1975. Khmer Rouge kill 1.7 -2 million Cambodians in the "Killing Fields."

Rwanda – 1994. 800,000 Hutu and Tutsi moderates hacked to death in 100 days, the quickest killing spree the world has ever seen since the Flood. Up to 500,000 women raped.

Bosnia – 1992. Serb "ethnic cleansing" kills 100,000 Bosnkiak and Croat civilians.

Darfur – 2013 – 300,000 Darfuri civilians murdered, two million displaced.

As of this writing, an estimated 650,000 are at risk in South Sudan. Thousands of Rohingya are

---

[80] United to End Genocide, Washington, DC 2015

stranded at sea, fleeing Burma. Boatloads of refugees embark on doomed journeys across the Mediterranean; many who make landfall are in miserable tent cities in a bankrupt Greece. The European Union squabbles over who will accept what is seen as the garbage of North Africa.

And so it goes.

Questioning God seems scary. He seems the only solid bedrock in a world of treacherous quicksand. We must recognize that examining the critical questions, exposing the dark to light, can in the end reaffirm our faith as stronger than before or lead to a new understanding of ourselves and mankind.

Chapter 23 The Psychology of Atheism

Atheism around the globe increased by 3% between 2005 and 2012.[81] China leads the world, with a whopping 47% of the populace reporting as non-believers. Japan is second with 31%, followed by the Czech Republic with 30% and France with 29% declaring themselves atheists.

There seems to be controversy about the Chinese number for several reasons, one being that Confucianism is not recognized as a religion. Formerly officially atheistic, policy has relaxed so that the 1978 constitution prohibits the state from enforcing any religious or non-religious policy at all.

In the United States, two thirds of atheists are men, with 38% between ages 18 and 29. 43% have a college degree.[82]

Anti-religious folks have not been shy about contributing to the literature. Often, the lines blur between the atheist, who avers God does not exist, the agnostic, who says he does not know, and the antitheist

---

[81] Win-Gallup International Global Index of Religiosity and Atheism - 2012
[82] Pew Research Center, October 9, 2012

who confines himself to the argument that religion in general is harmful to man. The antitheist opposes God without necessarily denying His existence. For over two centuries, their writings have ranged from the bitter diatribe of Robert Ingersoll to the essays of Richard Dawkins and Richard Hitchens, Penn Teller and Clarence Darrow.

In 1896, Ingersoll penned Why I Am An Agnostic, a raging indictment of God, if He exists, and Ingersoll doesn't want him to. Ingersoll makes several powerful arguments but undermines their effectiveness with caustic commentary. He observes that we inherit our opinions and attitudes: the son of a Muslim grows up to worship Allah. The Scotch are Calvinists and Irish are Catholic because their fathers were. Mom's religion is good enough for her daughter. Religion slowly evolves to reflect the times. These are all obvious points and hardly in dispute.

Ingersoll notes that simple stories and parables appropriate to the nation's agrarian past eventually gave way to more complex but equally abhorrent ideas. He goes on to attack the God of the Old Testament, whom he hates. He recites the litany of God's cruelty – babies butchered, women violated, old people slain. Mass genocide, drowning everyone including babies, women, children "because his mercy endureth forever." He offed the beasts and birds because "His loving kindness is all over his works."

Ingersoll has nothing but contempt for the God of Abraham. Pestilence and disease were His weapons, withholding the rain and starving His people. Ingersoll's wrath extends to the pulpit, where he condemns hellfire preachers who endorsed suffering and pain as suitable for heavenly reward whereas those who keep a happy home and are good citizens are doomed to hell.

He saves much of his ranting for The New Testament, which fares no better for Ingersoll, since the concept of eternal damnation and punishment are introduced and described. He says that "In the New Testament the malice of God is infinite and the hunger of his revenge eternal." Ingersoll mocks "the justice of God – the mercy of Christ." Descriptions of Hell stoked his hatred of religion and the Almighty. Ingersoll decries "idiotic Bible passages" as being so ridiculous people have deemed them "profoundly spiritual."

Pretty strong stuff. Suffice to say Ingersoll is not the flag bearer for the non-religious.

Clarence Darrow, the eminent attorney who defended schoolteacher John Scopes in the Monkey Trial as well as Leopold and Loeb in the child murder of Bobby Franks, wrote a Little Blue Book essay in 1929 also entitled Why I Am An Agnostic. He says that to believe in something, we must be able to picture it, and we cannot picture God. We can only grasp that He is a force. While an interesting observation, how this relates to agnosticism is not clear.

His narrative asks the question: Can any rational person believe that the Bible is anything but a human document?

Darrow points out that the various books were written by humans with "no knowledge of science, little knowledge of life, and were influenced by the barbarous morality of primitive times, and were grossly ignorant of most things that men know today." He observes that Genesis gives short shrift to the creation of the stars, a clear indication that the author had no conception of the stars or the heavens. The earth was the center of the universe. The stars were not very far above, mere adornments to the world. Darrow is of course accurate on this point and without divine inspiration no writer from those times would have thought any differently.

Darrow notes that the books of the Bible were written over a span of more than a thousand years, largely by unknown authors, and that taken as a whole the Bible is full of contradictions about life, morals, and the origin of things.

In short, Darrow tells us the Bible is an outmoded, obsolete and primitive text inspiring the fear of God, rather than the encouragement of skepticism and doubt in search of wisdom. He ends his discussion thusly:

"The modern world is the child of doubt and inquiry, as the ancient world was the child of fear and faith."

The true atheist is at a disadvantage: he affirms his belief in something that cannot be proven with the additional difficulty of having no articles of faith to pin his unbelief on. He has no miracles, dubious or not, to buttress his position. Indeed, faith is not an arrow in his quiver. We should examine why an individual would take the extra step into an illogical belief.

Antitheist and author Christopher Hitchens is credited for putting forth a variation of Occam's Razor (Hitchens' Razor) concerning religion: "What can be asserted without evidence can be dismissed without evidence." Why Hitchens is credited for saying this is a mystery as the statement itself is essentially meaningless. The assertion can be dismissed if that is the goal but the claim itself is not disproved.

Spokespersons for atheism often rely on faulty argument. Richard Dawkins, an atheist and emeritus fellow of New College, Oxford, said "The onus is on you to say why; the onus is not on the rest of us to say why not."

We can allow this grade school logic as a fair observation, but the difficulty with this and Hitchens' statement is that they can be turned around and used against the atheist. The nonbeliever makes a positive assertion that God does not exist. The only correct position that can be taken as a consequence of these statements, though, is agnosticism, or antitheism, as the logic goes nowhere towards proving the absence of God. What it does do is say something about the individual. In fact, it doesn't take a great deal of thought to realize the non-existence of God cannot be proven by any means whatever. Therefore we must look elsewhere to understand the atheist.

This argument is advanced again in a more recent work, *Why There is No God: Simple Responses to 20 Common Arguments for the Existence of God* by Armin Navabi. His lynchpin appears to be the same as Hitchens and Dawkins and offers nothing new.

Dan Barker's 2008 book *Godless: How an Evangelical Preacher Became One of America's Leading Atheists* is an interesting autobiographical work for two reasons. The stunning cover design shows Adam's hand from Michelangelo's Sistine Chapel ceiling reaching out to – no one. This has tremendous emotional impact. The second point of interest is a glimpse inside the mind of an evangelical preacher, a scary concept to many.

Writing about the paranormal, Sociology Professor Marcello Truzzi observed, "In science, the burden of proof falls upon the claimant; and the more extraordinary a claim, the heavier is the burden of proof demanded. The true skeptic takes an agnostic position, one that says the claim is not proved rather than disproved."[83] He goes on to state that the skeptic does not bear a burden of proof unless he claims disproof. This argument is intrinsically more logical than that of the atheist.

---

[83] On Pseudo-Skepticism. Zeletic Scholar 12/13, pp 3-4, 1987

Antitheism as promulgated by Dawkins is largely based on the intricacies of evolution and gene development. Author of *The Blind Watchmaker*, Dawkins argues against creationism and intelligent design. The problem is this: evolution as explained by Dawkins could be completely accurate, but tangential to the question of the existence of God. If we can postulate that God created the universe, why couldn't he have allowed life to develop through the evolutionary process? The universe itself is an evolutionary process from The Big Bang forward.

Atheism, though, is a reactionary position. Hostility to God, persons, ideas or things, likely because of negative occurrences in one's own life, or perhaps mental issues of whatever type, are likely causational. In the case of those initially raised in Christianity, it may be hostility to the Bible as evidenced by the writings of Ingersoll, perhaps a harsh upbringing by Bible-thumping parents. For those born of other faiths, there would be no reason to detest or be disturbed by the Bible any more than a Christian would become atheistic because of the Koran or the ravings of Ron Hubbard.

Another reason for atheism does not require a hostile personality, but a sensitive one. One cannot look at the terrible things that happen in life and go on happening, without wondering why this is allowed, especially with the concept of a loving God. Every thinking person has wondered this.

Barrels of ink have been used trying to explain how God can allow tragedy and heartache. The concept of "free will" is used as a defense, but it is a false explanation with little relevance. There is no definite cause and effect between suffering and free will. Babies starve, children are abused, accidents happen. The will of the victims plays no part.

When tragedy strikes, some draw closer to God for comfort, others turn away and lose whatever faith they may have had. An equally valid argument is that God created us and left. Perhaps He ceased to exist, which would mean He was something less than the conventional definition we have ascribed to Him.

Throughout much of history, Jews have had compelling reason to feel abandoned by Yahweh. The history of Judaism is a history of difficulty, repression and enslavement, culminating in the near-genocide of the Holocaust. Certainly some lost their God. Yet Judaism not only survives but thrives, although their numbers are small. Oppression has sustained the religion, often all the Jews have had for comfort and spiritual sustenance since the physical was so often denied. Under horrific conditions of existence, the Jewish belief in a better heaven than afforded other religions is understandable, if illogical. Tradition, ritual, and a strong sense of history are powerful forces.

We see things virtually daily that test our beliefs. A very sensitive, altruistic person may well feel the God he has been taught to believe in is nowhere to be found.

If there was a God, he rejected or lost interest in man. A few years ago, in China, an earthquake in an outlying region did little damage except to all the schools, which collapsed while classes were in session. Government aid was too slow or nonexistent. For days parents dug frantically with their hands through the collapsed rubble of elementary schools, as cell phones rang faintly from inside. After awhile the ringing stopped. It turned out that little or no mortar had been used in the buildings' construction, and criminal charges were brought against local officials and the builders. Did God watch this agony passively? If He did, what does it say about Him? Does He want, as Protestants insist, a personal relationship with each of us? It would have been too late for the little Chinese tots.

We can cite endless examples but the point is made. There is no good way to reconcile a loving God with these events, no matter how much is said about free will and self-determination. It is and will remain a problem for organized religion of all faiths, and perhaps the only thing upon which an atheist can truly hang his unbelief. It is a powerful argument.

Chapter 24 The Morality of Disbelief

No one would relish standing in front of a kindergarten class and telling all the five year olds there is no Santa Claus, no need to confess transgressions to the Bearded One before getting a slew of presents at the end of the year.

In America and elsewhere clergy are respected in society. They are normally well-intended people wont to help others and guide them spiritually through difficult times, sickness and death. They officiate at happy occasions like weddings and baptisms, bar mitzvahs and first communions. They participate in family milestones, whether celebrating or comforting, providing a positive spiritual compass. They are respected and admired, for the most part. Their churches, synagogues, and other religious organizations participate in community service, aiding the poor and disabled, ministering to prisoners, the downtrodden, feeding the hungry and sheltering the battered.

These are positive things. Religion is often a positive concept. Priests, ministers, rabbis – they are good folks.

The atheist, antitheist or agnostic has no church, no community organization. He does not participate in positive or uplifting actions for the community on an organized level. To announce to the world one does not believe in God has negative connotations.

To the undecided, then, the half-hearted churchgoer who may earnestly seek truth, there is great pressure to believe what may seem unbelievable or at least doubtful. This pressure is called faith. It is a bad thing not to have, we are told. There is a moral wind blowing the hesitant towards belief in spite of nagging doubt. This is an incredibly strong force and allows false credence to what otherwise might be dismissed as nonsense. Standards of proof in any courtroom or classroom are ignored. Rumor, hearsay, anonymous writings, incredible claims are held as gospel - literally.

We support the do-good activities of our churches and synagogues. We want to believe in Santa Claus. We want the Easter Bunny to hop on down the bunny trail. We want our kids to believe, at least until an age of reason.

Most of us trust our parents. If they were religious, we are going to feel betrayal if we stray from the fold. We nourish on the mother's milk of parental beliefs. As youngsters, Bible stories may have been a center point of family activity or church participation. We accepted these treasured stories basically without question. It takes a lot to change beliefs ingrained from childhood.

A Roman Catholic is normally not as familiar with the books of the Bible as other Christians. While the gospels of Matthew, Mark, Luke and John are read at Mass, the bulk of the books are not studied. This is simply because there is no need. It is the Catholic belief that the current Pope is the interpreter of religious dogma and when he speaks or writes *ex cathedra* he is putting forth infallible and true doctrine, straight from the source, so to speak. Roman Catholicism relies on Matthew 16:18 for this privilege, quoting Jesus:

"I say to you that you are Peter, and upon this rock I will build My church, and the gates of hell shall not prevail against it. I will give you the keys of the kingdom of heaven, and whatever you bind on earth shall have been bound in heaven, and whatever you loose on earth shall have been loosed in heaven."

Relying on this passage, there is little need to study the old texts for truth or enlightenment, and, as a result, the Bible is really unfamiliar to much of the Roman Catholic laity. It is interesting, then, to gauge the reaction of Catholics when they do peruse the Bible for the first time. For many, it is as reading Aesop's fables. The more fantastic claims and stories evoke an incredulous reaction. Irrespective of the above, the 1869 Council of the Vatican as well as Pope Leo XIII, Pope Benedict XV and Pope Pius XII have averred the inerrancy of the Bible, holding it as sacred and under the spirit and guidance of the Holy Spirit. Later, though, the Second Vatican Council in 1965 apparently allowed some wiggle room concerning scientific Biblical pronouncements, limiting the infallibility of the work to spiritual matters: faith, morality and salvation. This was supported by the Secretariat for Ecumenical and Interreligious Affairs at the United States Conference of Catholic Bishops in 1999. And there the matter essentially lies with the Roman Catholic Church.

Protestants, raised on the Bible's revered tales since early childhood, have no such reaction and little reservations for the most part. What is rooted in childhood is accepted as an adult. Ongoing debates between Protestant sects are confined to interpretation of the book, whether literal or figurative, but the stories and lore are basically unquestioned. Noah built a giant ark and in a week stuffed seven specimens of every living clean animal into it, plus food and other necessaries. God created earth's vegetation before he fashioned the stars. And so on. To challenge is to offend, to somehow vaguely move from the righteous and well-meaning to the heretical and immoral.

When we watch an entertaining movie, we automatically go into a state called suspension of disbelief. We are swept along by stories fantastic, tales of derring-do and wonder that we know could never be real. But we're on for the ride, and are thrilled, scared, moved to tears. And so it goes. By suspending our powers of reason, we are rewarded with entertainment and emotional experience. As a result, it is often difficult or impossible for someone raised with the Bible to evaluate the material dispassionately.

When we hear the solemn words intoned onscreen by the likes of John Huston or Charlton Heston, they are impressive and carry the ring of authority.

Chapter 25   Who Created Whom?

Perhaps nowhere in the history of the written word is there a more profoundly egotistical statement than found in the Old Testament, Genesis 1:27:

"And God created man in His own image, in the image of God He created him, male and female He created them."

Did He? God must have a sense of humor to let that one get by.

Not long after in Genesis 6-9, the same author[84] describes the Great Flood, when God destroyed pretty much everything and everybody because mankind, despite having been created in God's image, had become wickedly sinful, all save Noah and his immediate family.

A bit further on, Genesis 19:24 relates the destruction of Sodom and Gomorrah, as the Lord could not find even ten righteous men in those cities.

Clearly, something is wrong. Either Genesis 1:27 is a flight of wishful fancy or God made a mistake. We've discussed this in a previous chapter. If He made a mistake, then He doesn't fit our conception of Him.

---

[84] Widely accepted as Moses

Since the author of Genesis was a human being, it was much more likely his error, perhaps a bit of puffery.

We can see in just those few pages there is really not much chance God created man in His own image.

All these words were written when the earth was the center of a very small universe, and man's ego could afford to believe he was the center of attention.

On balance, it is more likely man created God in his own image instead.

It has happened time after time, in civilization after civilization, rudimentary or sophisticated.

Chapter 26 What Does It All Mean?

Belief or non-belief in God can depend a great deal on what we want from Him. We have looked at various aspects of belief: cultural, psychological, historical, cosmological. We have given ourselves simple tools to weed out the superfluous, the silly, the perverse, the elitist. These tools allow us perspective, so that we may focus a bit better on what the Creator may be like.

Concerning man's historical relationship with God and the character of man's religions, we can make some tentative conclusions:

-   Man will always invent God, whether He is really there or not.
-   Man will ascribe human motivations and thinking to God.
-   Man will always believe God is intensely interested in him.
-   Man will always invent stories and false logic to align God with his particular ethnic, social, or political group, to his benefit and often the detriment of others.

- Man will usually believe God wants him to wage battle against others, carrying the banner of a specific belief. Man will kill others who believe differently under the delusion God wants him to.
- The Bible and other religious texts are works of man. They contain multitudes of contradictions, scientific errors, beautiful poetry, fantastic stories, nonsense, morality tales, inspired passages, extraneous material, romantic sagas, lilting prose, pornography, incest[85] and third person hearsay. They are often so contradictory and abstruse they foster intense and unending study without possibility of resolution. Man cannot view these writings with clarity, because those who try are normally emotionally invested and strain for consistency when there is none. As an example, it is often pointed out how the Old and New Testaments are remarkably consistent, when in actuality they are wildly inconsistent on basic matters such as the character of God. Man focuses on the trivial, such as a vague continuity of lineage.
- Most religions believe in an earthly link in the person of a Holy individual, whether prophet

---

[85] As when Lot's daughters got their father tanked and had sex with him. Such was the pedigree of the Moabites and the Ammonites.

or part God such as Jesus, Mohammad, Moses
or whomever.
-   The character of religion is directly related to
    the ethnic, economic and educationally
    accomplished groups that espouse it.
-   The more educated man is, the less likely he
    is to believe in God.
-   The more affluent man is, the less likely he is
    to believe in God.
-   Permissive and entitled societies such as that
    of the United States become less religious
    over time.
-   These societies, while declining in religiosity,
    nonetheless foster two dichotomous religious
    archetypes: megachurches, which are heavily
    social, emphasizing earthly reward and
    deemphasizing dogma, and very conservative
    right wing groups, such as Orthodox Jews and
    the Amish. The former tend to be
    evolutionary, the latter insular and reactionary
    to the society.
-   Atheism is an irrational belief, as there is not
    a shred of evidence to favor it. Therefore it a
    reactionary view whose adoption is colored
    by emotional and/or intellectual disability.
-   Those who profess atheism are viewed as
    being of lesser moral character, even by
    agnostics and antitheists.

In summary, man's religious endeavors, imperfect historical records and gropings for God are less than useful in determining much of anything concerning His existence or character. None of the above has any correlation whatever with the basic questions asked in Chapter 1.

Thus, the question of whether God exists must be examined in light of our other investigations.

In terms of cosmological inquiry, the universe itself has proven more complex, more elegant, incredibly vast, and increasingly more wondrous as we have continued to unlock its secrets. Our growing ability to understand the workings of the cosmos reveal still more complex, subtle workings, and this ability does nothing to conclude that it all happened by itself.

The now-accepted belief that the universe had a beginning and will probably end in cold darkness does little to foster or deny the existence of God, especially as we do not know if we are but one cosmos in an array of multiple universes. We may be one Big Bang in an unending series of Big Bangs and Big Crunches, although that now seems mathematically unlikely, as we have seen. We also know that time itself may not have existed before the Big Bang, and that time can be manipulated, at least in a single direction, and viewed in the other direction.

We do not know what was, before creation of this universe, if anything. We know some of what is, and speculate about what will be. So what can we conclude about God, then?

On balance, the majesty of the universe implies a creator. It is not a certainty, it is not proof, but is more than just a possibility.

Chapter 27 Conclusion

We know that life will spring up under all sorts of conditions, here and throughout the universe, if we push aside our egos and allow for the mathematically obvious. We see the wonders of creation in fantastic creatures here on and in the earth, and in the sea and skies. Our minds may accept random evolution as the artist painting the masterpiece, the blind watchmaker at his eternal workbench, but our eyes and hearts tell us otherwise, that something beyond our ken created this artistry, or at least set it all in motion.

We gaze up at the clouds and blue sky and are unable to separate our emotions from logic, incapable of dispassionately resolve our dilemma.   It's the human condition.

And that's all right.

We gaze at a wind-swept ocean on a brisk fall day in wonder, smell the fresh sea air, watch the spray catch the light, see the rainbow above the waves. We hear the laughter of a child, the faint backdrop of cicadas on a soft summer evening, the whisper of the wind as it moves the grain in golden waves across the fields. At night, we gaze upward as silver-tinged clouds slide across the stars, draw curtains across the moon.

We know in our hearts it's not all math and logic.

I am a pilot by avocation, and as I look out the cockpit window at the majesty of the clouds and play tag with those giant white pylons, I look down at the aching beauty of the earth and water below and feel a closeness with a Creator. This is the nature of man. He can reason, but reason won't solve his problem or soothe his mind.

Logic and science haven't yet given us the answer, and may never tell us what we seek. We look inward, look to our hearts, where the knowledge may already lie.

In the end, it's all so personal and intimate, and so it should be.

www.ingramcontent.com/pod-product-compliance
Lightning Source LLC
Chambersburg PA
CBHW071002040426
42443CB00007B/616